Parish Celebrations

A REFLECTIVE GUIDE FOR LITURGY PLANNING

Dennis J. Geaney, OSA

Dolly Sokol

TWENTY-THIRD
PUBLICATIONS
Mystic, Connecticut

ISBN: 0-89622-190-3
Library of Congress Catalog Card Number: 83-70621

Edited by Kathleen Connolly
Designed by John G. van Bemmel
Cover by Kathy Michalove

CONTENTS

FOREWORD

I like this book very much. Dennis Geaney and Dolly Sokol focus on the real issues of worship that are just emerging from the whirlwind of "doing things" and "changing things" that followed immediately, and necessarily somewhat thoughtlessly, in the wake of Vatican II. Now that we have the luxury of some perspective, we are able to take a fresh look. We are beginning now to understand that the Vatican II call is a call to radical conversion, a call to accept the restored vision of the church as all God's people equally responsible for the total mission of the church in the world, a call to think differently about sacraments and to do them differently, quite differently. The book helps us to take that deeper look, to make that deeper commitment.

The book makes it clear that if we, as church, take this call seriously and make it happen, we are going to march creatively into the next millenium. If we do not, we shall continue with that ho-hum custodial care and minimal maintenance that we are so much bored with today.

Dennis Geaney and Dolly Sokol offer the kind of fresh insights that alone can lead to genuine renewal and conversion. For instance, 1) Sunday Mass belongs to the whole parish assembly. It can no longer be thought of or celebrated as if it were the possession only of priests and other special ministers. 2) Sunday Mass gets to be truly life-giving to the degree that it becomes the warm and inviting human experience it is meant to be. 3) Sunday Mass will continue to be a sterile and self-serving enterprise unless it gradually transforms members of the assembly into disciples genuinely committed to gospel values and to service of others.

This is an excellent book for parishes that really want to break the bread of life for their own members but even more for those who are outside.

Dennis and Dolly dare to expose the best kept secret of liturgy: The parish Sunday Mass explodes into an experience of the presence of the risen Lord when it becomes a deliberate and warm sharing of the members of the assembly.

This book offers many practical suggestions for making the parish Sunday Mass a truly life-giving celebration and the parish a life-giving community. These suggestions do not come from the head or from the academy, but from the rich and creative experience of both authors who work in quite different parish settings.

Eugene A. Walsh, S.S.

PREFACE

When there's a wedding banquet on Saturday night at the American Legion Hall in Calumet City, it flourishes with human activity. The toasts have been offered; the tables have been cleared; the young and middle aged are beginning to get into the polka with a passion. The older folks are content to chat about good times in the old neighborhood, exchange bits of current gossip, or admire their relatives gyrating on the dance floor. The bartenders are in constant motion. If the Lord was serious when he said, "The kingdom of God is like a wedding feast," we are in the midst of a Polish American version of the kingdom. We are at a noneucharistic liturgy, or agape. The love is almost palpable.

This scene has something in common with another dining room in the back of Vicki's Tavern, Steve's Lounge, the VFW, or the same American Legion Hall. This time I am here to break bread with families after we have been to the cemetery burying a member of the family. As we mill around and finally sit, we talk about children growing up, jobs lost and found, a family member leaving from O'Hare Airport for another part of the country. As we pass the food and chat, we know without being able to talk about it that in this sharing of food we are in the Emmaus restaurant, experiencing the breaking of the bread.

The bread of the American Legion Hall is being transformed by the death of a loved one, a love we cannot put into words. The caring and sharing as the food is being passed in family style is tangible in these familiar surroundings where people grieve so well. It is here as well as in church that we can fittingly follow the command of the Lord to take and eat, and experience the breaking of the bread that climaxes the love feast that began on the first night of the wake.

Through the wedding banquet and the after-the-cemetery brunch we have images or symbols that capture what Sunday liturgies are meant to be. The Lord used simple events that revolved around food and enjoying the company of family and friends to speak to us about his dying and rising, the Easter event. He grounded his description of the kingdom in family situations, preparing and serving meals, sweeping the floor for a lost coin, farming and fishing, and in employee/employer relationships.

The wedding banquet and the funeral brunch are celebrative events marking significant turning points in family histories. The wedding celebrates the past histories of each family and points to the future with unabashed hope. The funeral brunch celebrates love that is as real as the shared bread that is passed across the table, accompanied by the retelling of family stories and the touching gestures of care. The principal celebrant of the first is the couple and of the second, the living memory of the deceased.

These two liturgies are orchestrated by liturgy planning teams: the wedding usually by the mother of the bride, the funeral brunch by the spouse or nearest of kin. At the wedding banquet the roles are well defined by the bridal gowns and the rented tuxedos. At the funeral brunch, vestments serve no purpose. In both instances the emphasis is on peer ministry. Everyone in each of the assemblies is caring for everyone. The love that radiates in the hall is larger than the couple, and the love at Vicki's Tavern is larger than the memory of the deceased. These are simply the occasions that bring together and heighten the love that captures the interlocking histories of all the people in the rooms. Through their faith, hope, and love they become in these moments clearly who they are: a holy people.

These two events are used to help us grasp the possibilities for our Sunday liturgies. Sunday liturgies are designed to help us celebrate the ordinary events of daily living by putting them in the context of the ritual action we call the Mass, that is, the making present of the dying and rising of the Lord. While every Sunday is meant to be an earthly approximation of the heavenly banquet and the breaking of the bread, we are not able to have the same kind of celebrations that we have at the American Legion or Vicki's Tavern. We cannot rise to the occasion Sunday after Sunday to dramatize our sniffles, our lumbago, a temporary job loss, a good report card, or winning a lottery. The parish is not the same kind of extended family as the family celebrating a wedding or a death. Our contact with most of the congregation may not go beyond the walls of the church, but we do cherish and celebrate the faith in the dying and rising of Jesus that brings us together. With all these differences we do see the wedding banquet and the funeral brunch as helpful symbols for liturgy planners, musicians, readers, presiders, preachers, and communion ministers.

In this book we are addressing ourselves to those in leadership roles in the parish, namely, those who assume leadership responsibility for the development of the liturgical life of the parish and those concerned with specific liturgical roles: presiders, ministers of the word and the bread, greeters, sacristans, planners. We are also addressing ourselves to those indirectly involved in the liturgy who have a bearing on its directions: the parish council, the finance committee, the building and grounds committee, the secretarial and janitorial staff. In our more sanguine moments we fantasize the circle growing larger as ripples on a pond so that the Omega point would be reached wherein everyone is vitally concerned with the direction of the liturgy and becomes caught up in the dialogue. When we disembark from our flight of fancy we find ourselves addressing the staff and liturgical ministers. We hope in the process to find ways of involving those on the outer rim by questionnaires, surveys, or feedback sessions that keep the members of the inner circle from talking to themselves and assuming that they are the assembly.

While we recognize that there is an infrastructure of traditions, laws, and decrees coming from the Vatican and from national and diocesan legislative bodies, and while we are aware that these mediate the tradition, we claim just as strongly that the local assembly is the church, which mediates the tradition and within this context has an autonomy that needs to be developed as well as respected.

We have pooled our experiences as associate pastors, liturgists, and social activists to speak to parish ministers—priests, deacons, professional lay and religious staff members, and particularly members of liturgical committees—about our common understandings and experiences. Since Dolly has two fulltime jobs—as a member of the pastoral team of Ford City Catholic Center Parish and a staff member of the Chicago Office for Divine Worship—and I have only one—associate pastor of St. Victor Parish, Calumet City, Illinois—I choose to be the chronicler. Dolly brings to her role as liturgist at Ford City her master's degree in drama and her theological studies at the Catholic Theological Union. My contact with the North American liturgical movement dates to my coming-out article on liturgy and life in the twenty-fifth anniversary issue of *Orate Fratres* in 1951.[1]

No book is original; it draws from the heritage of the trailblazers of the past and from our contemporaries on the cutting edge. Therefore, we express our indebtedness to the pioneers of the American liturgical movement, and especially to the past and present members of our parish staffs, the liturgical committee members and liturgical ministers of St. Victor's and Ford City. They had the courage to test the insights of the scholars and adapt them to Catholic Middle America. In the final analysis it is the liturgical assemblies, the people themselves, who validate what we have to offer in this book. We also wish to ackknowledge and thank Francis Kalies for patiently and graciously typing and retyping this manuscript.

1

ASSEMBLIES DIFFER

Modern transportation has done much for liturgical education. When we vacation in the Smokies, visit Aunt Nellie in Colorado, or go on an excursion bus to Washington, D.C. that requires a weekend stay, we see how the rest of the country celebrates the liturgy. We compare our home church with the resort church on the shore or lake that caters to tourists and features a familiar second collection. If we are touring the nation's Capitol and worship at the Shrine of the Immaculate Conception, our entire American Catholic history flows through our responses in word and song. We experience a sense of majesty and being at the center of the American branch of the Roman Catholic Church. A visit to our roots in rural Iowa may bring us in prayerful relationship with a holy octogenerian celebrant who brings us into contact with the sacred through pre-Vatican II forms. These experiences may affirm what we do well at home and also create a healthy dissatisfaction with some of the ways we pray, which leads us to investment in change.

Probably the greatest symbol of liturgical change in this country is the moving van on an interstate highway. It may be the chaircouple of the liturgical committee of Sacred Heart Parish, Dearborn, Michigan, being relocated in North Carolina. In a town with a small Catholic population they will find a ready reception to their fresh energies, if they are willing to accept the prayer experience of the locals as genuine and their attitude is not patronizing. This book is similar to the moving van. It is simply attempting to move experiences people have had from one parish or diocese to another via the printed word. We cannot travel to your parish to conduct a workshop, but we can present some possibilities for a more prayerful celebrative service.

Who are we to change the liturgy? This book is not about changing the liturgical books of the church that give us the script and the direction of their use. It is concerned with a more fruitful way of using these books to improve the quality of prayer and community life.

Who Decides?

No one can tell a group of people how to pray, how to ritualize, how to celebrate. Prayer must be the unique expression of a community at this moment in its history. No pope, bishop, theologian, or liturgist knows what is best for us; this is the decision of the community. But who is the community? How can a group of worshipers make a decision? Are communities of worshipers like riderless horses, or are they like Topsy, "I just happened"?

Every gathering of people has a character. It can be studied as theater, as people move with moods and movements from beginning to end. It may begin with solitary ticket buyers lining up for their seats as they anticipate an exciting or boring performance. As the program engages or fails to engage theatergoers, feelings are transmitted and shared by themselves and performers alike. At an opera or play, the people may enter its depths in awed, breathless silence, and at the curtain call there is a release that says that we were becoming one with each other without consciously acknowledging each other's presence.

If the performance fails to generate feelings that strike the deep chords of our psyche and proves to be discordant with our experience, there may be shared feelings that unite the body in protest. More likely the feelings will express themselves in sullen silence, a form of passive aggression. The point we are making is simple: every assembly has a unique character. It assumes a personality that may be flexible or very rigid. Our belief in the Spirit encourages us to believe that however ossified that corporate personality has become, it is capable of moving to progressively deeper levels in which each person is enriched and the totality of the enrichment of each becomes a force that sustains and supports the inner thrust of all. The contrary may also happen. Destructive feelings can be generated and lead people to display the worst that is in them.

This applies to liturgy as it does to theater or a political rally. However, in parish worship we may be inclined to assume that the folks in the congregation or assembly are mute spectators who take their cues from the altar rather than from each other, as though the assembly had no mind of its own. If the people have no desire to sing, Alex Peloquin or the St. Louis Jesuits will not be able to move them. If the presiding celebrant encourages them to express their concern for each other in a warm, loving gesture of friendship, the people may refuse or make an empty gesture which mocks the purpose. While the assembly may not have the leverage to initiate, it can affirm or deny what is being expected of it. It can dictate with its feet.

Parish Liturgies Differ

What makes liturgies in one parish different from those in another? Is it the pastor, a dominant associate, a liturgy committee, or leader of the assembly who determines the style and response of the liturgy? Is it another spectator event in a consumer society? If we look closely at the different liturgies of a particular parish on any weekend, we will find different styles and different responses from assemblies that have the same cast and the same script. We need to develop a sharp eye for detecting the centers of influence that initiate change.

The five o'clock Saturday evening parish Mass across the country seems to attract similar constituencies. It attracts older parishioners, people who have a compulsion to clear the deck of all obligations at the first opportunity, people who have worked all week and like Sunday for themselves, people who work on Sundays, and people who will be traveling, picnicking or entertaining on a particular Sunday. The weather forecaster can fill the church on a Saturday evening with a threatening weather report for Sunday. The five o'clock Massgoers tend to come early and fill the church, beginning with the rear pews. A few will have a built-in alarm that goes off when they feel that in God's eyes they absolved themselves of their duty to him. They feel that the responsibility for their exit after communion rests with the presiding celebrant, who is needlessly prolonging God's service.

It is easy for ministers to be judgmental and imply by tone of voice and body gestures that God is dissatisfied with the congregation. The first approach to the late Saturday afternoon congregation is respect for their integrity and fidelity. It is too easy to be judgmental and conclude that they are present because it is an odious obligation. National Opinion Research Institute and Gallup polls do not substantiate this judgment.

A later Saturday evening Mass in parishes that cannot accommodate all the Saturday evening worshipers with one Mass finds a more relaxed assembly well-spaced in the church. For the most part they have had their evening meal; some have their favorite television programs ahead of them, or they may be going to a party from which they will be arriving home late and want to enjoy a long sleep on Sunday.

The early Sunday morning worshipers have a different face. At seven or eight o'clock a small number of people

are scattered in a church large enough to make them feel like the Christian remnant. The early morning Mass people are habitual early risers. A less crowded church allows them more breathing room. It is the best Mass for people who have bouts of claustrophobia.

People generally form an attachment to a particular place where they stand, sit, and kneel. They become comfortable in their place and find it easier to pray there, whether it is front, back, side, or middle. Since place facilitates concentration or centering, as a rosary does without hands and lips, their choice must be respected.

A liturgist fresh out of school who embraces a theology of liturgy as an expression of community might be inclined to manipulate these people into a tight cadre close to the altar. The people at the early Mass are usually older people who have seen pastors, associates, and other staff people come and go. They have built the buildings, supported the staff, seen programs start and fail and staff members leave their failures behind them as they move to the next assignment. The early risers deserve to be respected. Each has a story to tell. It may be the occasion of being at the first Mass in the present church building fifty years ago after having worshiped in a frame building at the bottom of the hill as a small child. The liturgist, whose vocation it is to orchestrate the overarching symbols of the community, must listen to these stories in which their symbols are imbedded.

The early morning Mass is shorter for a number of reasons. Whether there is no singing because there has been no response to singing in the past or because the parish cannot afford an organist for this Mass, matters little. There is all-around acceptance that singing will be at a minimum. The Irish immigrant with a history of personal piety and unrefined aesthetic liturgical taste has been a factor in the development of the liturgical style of the American church. This stems from the penal days when a priest could be drawn and quartered for offering Mass. If it was to be done, it was to be done quickly behind locked doors.

The Poles, Germans, and other Eastern and Southern European immigrants had richer liturgical histories, but their inability to speak English on arrival and so to capture church leadership positions unfortunately gave the Irish an advantage. One of the unfortunate by-products is the in-and-out mentality that a few genuflections and signs of the cross fulfill one's obligation. While this may not be the motivation for the ancestors of the Irish today, habit endures. Customs are institutionalized, demanding tolerance and patience.

The population of each of the succeeding Sunday morning Masses tends to be larger and younger. The generalization of younger and older often equated with liberal and conservative, change and non-change, is a facile dichotomy that may be fallacious and an easy pitfall. The folk Mass, for example, was introduced in the sixties to attract young people who it was assumed were turned off by the traditional silent liturgies. Almost from the beginning, folk Masses attracted older as well as very elderly people. In the next decade it was no longer called a folk

Mass but was assimilated into the regular parish schedule.

Assemblies with an ethnic or racial history will be influenced by customs and thought patterns that have filtered into parish practice. While Black parishes are not any more alike than White parishes, we do find patterns. In southern Louisiana we have Black parishes that strive to preserve their liturgies intact as a way of preserving their Black cultural heritage in the bayou country. In northern cities we find old Black parishes that fight change because they do not want to go back to the noisy Baptist church which they left in the thirties for the quiet Latin Mass. At the other end of the spectrum are Black parishes like St. Mark's in Cincinnati, which tries to integrate African origins. It brings together the Black American experience and the best theological and liturgical studies to spell a joyful celebration with a gospel choir that brings people at the Sunday noon Mass to a profound community experience of the Lord. No one looks at a watch.

These observations about our Sunday liturgies are simply made to reinforce a single point. The assembly itself influences the quality of the liturgy and is the final arbiter of whether the staff and liturgy committee are on the right track. It is a devout wish that the assembly will feel a sense of its own power and find a fruitful way of dialoguing with the presider, other ministers, and liturgical planners. It is the assembly that is the gathered church in which the Lord reveals his presence. The Spirit does not come to us simply through the ministers at the altar as the performers at a stage theatrical. The risen Lord becomes present through the faith of the entire assembly, not simply through the eucharistic narrative recited by the presider.

The Daily Mass Assembly

While the daily Mass is not festive, it may be more communal than we suspect. During a period of convalescence from a coronary, I was asked to preside at a daily Mass each morning. The assembly was twenty-five elderly people, mostly women, in a side chapel. As the days and weeks went on, I found that we formed a nonverbal community of support for each other. They brought their old age and loneliness and I, my post-coronary depression to the altar. It was celebrative in the context of the paschal mystery.

On both sides of the altar we found in our brokenness that the risen Christ was our common source of hope. We found in each other an inner strength to continue in the struggle. The eucharist was the catalyst for our being a community and finding this Christ in the assembly. It was not music but common pain that gave the tension that good music provides, that enlarged our faith, buttressed our hope, and was expressed in love in our eye contact.

At St. Victor's daily seven o'clock Mass it is the vigorous handshake of peace by the two adult servers and the presider with everyone in the church that binds people into a caring community of believers. It is this symbol that saves the liturgy from simply being people in private prayer and private communion with other private pray-ers in the church at the same time.

As a church we have yet to face the issue of the Mass as a Sunday, rather than a daily, celebration. We may still wish to retain daily Mass but we should not foreclose the discussion without offering communal prayer services and the liturgy of the hours as options. With a shortage of priests, it seems that we might be in a position to turn over the presidency of communal prayer and worship to the lay people who have experience in prayer and ministering at the altar.

Our Response to Change

In this book change is seen as being open to creative possibilities for other ways to pray and celebrate. We are interested in continuity with the present and recent past. While we have a need to reflect on and cherish what worked well for us in our childhood and adulthood, we cannot allow ourselves to become stagnant in our community prayer. While we revere our childhood religious experiences and symbols, these powerful early beliefs need to find expression in our present culture and in our present living situation. At the same time we need to see them as opening up new vistas as we experience life in a new way in the present era of our life and culture. We take our cue from Jesus: "I have not come to destroy but to fulfill."

Our response to change is a key category in liturgical understanding. One of the assumptions we can make about change is to type people as change or non-change people. Some of the stereotypes are: Young are open to change and elders are not; working class people in old neighborhoods are less open to change than affluent suburbanites; the poor are closed and the intellectuals are open; conservatives are rigid and liberals are flexible. When these stereotypes become mindsets of the leaders of the assembly, then the assembly becomes boxed in and can only act through passive or open aggression. They are being treated as categories rather than persons.

How change takes place is basic to any understanding of liturgy. One of our basic assumptions is that while change itself is neutral and can be destructive as well as constructive, we live in a dynamic culture that evokes change in one's self-understanding of what it means to be human. While philosophers, psychologists, and sociologists theorize on the shift and novelists and journalists tell the story, we can breathe and feel, if not articulate, the change in our understandings of world, God, and self.

Since liturgy is a prayerful response to our human longings, then it must change if it is to reflect how people experience today what it means to them to be human. If our liturgical expressions have not changed, it may mean that they still respond to our childhood understanding of life. When our prayer does not respond to our adult life, it becomes dull and boring rather than responsive to life. By no means does this mean that every liturgical change in the past two decades has been a response to the deepest thrust of our human experience. We may have sold what was profound for something gimmicky and frilly.

Whether change is constructive or destructive, forward, backward, or lateral depends upon how well the assembly and especially its appointed leaders perceive what evokes the holy in our ever-emerging culture. While change itself is neutral, it is not an excuse for no change. If we accept the fact that we are moving through history and see culture as always evolving, never static, then our liturgy, which is an expression of a people living in a certain culture at a certain period of history, must always be in a process of evolving with the culture.

The American Catholic parish may be predominantly White, Black, Hispanic, or Oriental; affluent, middle class, or poor; suburban, urban, or inner-city. It may be in the Northeast, Southeast, Midwest, Southwest, West, or Northwest. The diocese, area, or parish may be labled conservative, middle of the road, or liberal, but within these are individuals who by their uniqueness defy all labeling. In spite of our diversity we are all pilgrims sharing the same faith and want to move forward together in the prayer of praise and thanksgiving in our Sunday liturgies. Our hope is that the prayer of our assembly can tap the underground stream of our tradition or Catholicity where we experience our oneness in Christ through whom we pray to the Father.

Questions for Reflection and Discussion

1. When you have celebrated liturgy in a parish other than your own, what did you notice about the liturgy that was different from your parish? What was your evaluation of it? Would that celebration fit your parish community? Why or why not?

2. What is the character of each of your parish's weekend Masses? What are the people like? How can you help them to pray and celebrate better?

3. What is the character of your daily Masses? Are they communal celebrations?

4. Does our parish's liturgical life respond to the adult lives of our parishioners or only to a childhood spirituality?

2

THE SPIRITUALITY
OF THE ASSEMBLY

At the 9:30 and 12:30 Sunday Masses at St. Victor, we hold hands as we sing the Our Father. Without waiting for the nod of the presider, people enthusiastically reach out for the hands of the people on both sides. It is obviously a joyous experience and may be even in the category of a religious experience when one is holding the hand of a person he or she is not accustomed to associate with. Other parishioners have a spirituality that causes them to avoid these Masses as they would a plague. They see God coming to them in a tiny whisper rather than the noisy demonstration of a relationship that they see as more gimmicky than real. The handshake of peace brings the same kind of mixed reaction. For some it is the visible wave of love that is flowing like a current and uniting people in a community of love. To others it is a painful exercise in mock friendliness interfering with communion with the Lord and spiritual communion with the assembly. In between these firmly held opposites is a silent majority who can swing or be swayed by the more vocal or demonstrative.

Each parish tends toward an identifiable style, even though it strives to be pluralistic and adapt itself to particular assemblies. In Boston the Paulist Center is known for a long break between the Liturgy of the Word and the Liturgy of the Eucharist during which people can mill around and renew weekly acquaintances. The practice is now deeply imbedded in the assembly's understanding of itself. Once the character of an assembly has been determined it can hardly be changed by decrees from outside without a trauma.

Styles Change

Each assembly has a style of worship of its own because it has a spirituality of its own. People go to a certain church or Mass because it suits them, and at the same time they are being further shaped by the spirituality of that particular assembly. In the decade following Vatican II we approached liturgical change with a fireman's axe. The pre-Vatican II spirituality had to be gutted before the structure could be reshaped to the image and likeness of the reformers. In the late sixties we were still in an authoritarian church, and the old was ripped out simply on orders from on high and the new imposed because the orders came from the same high command. When changes were implemented without arduous preparation of both minister and assembly, the authentic spirituality of individuals and communities was trampled upon.

An authoritarian approach to change in the decade of the eighties quickly backfires. What we need are the tools for understanding the spirituality of a particular worshiping community and how people have come to relate to it. The community may be willing to look at other possibilities if their present spirituality is respected. Each person comes to the assembly as a response to childhood religious practices. The understanding of a religious belief and practice in one's home, the tradition of one's parish church, the decade in which one was born, which determined the religious feelings of parents and how religion was taught, will be decisive in the assessment of one's spirituality. A study of Catholic youth reveals that parents who had children after Vatican II when they began to see God as a loving God rather than a demanding God raised their children with a different spirituality than did parents of the previous generation.[1] Spirituality is also shaped by crisis situations: death, illnesses, separations, successes and failures with peers in school or at work.[2]

Regina Kuehn

Identifying the Spirituality of Liturgical Ministers

Since staff members and the parish liturgical committee are in leadership roles, they need to look at their own religious experiences and see how their own spirituality and prayer life have been shaped. Without this conscious reflection we may be giving double messages. At one level we may be encouraging people to pray communally while our own unexamined prayer life is still at the "Jesus and me" level. A pastor and professor of systematic theology at a non-denominational school of theology told this story about himself. Robbers broke into the rectory, tied him up, bagged his head, and left him with the feeling that he might be shot. He then piously made the perfect act of contrition that he had been taught in the third grade.

We need to identify these stories of God—the childhood, adolescent, and adult experiences that have shaped our lives. We do this in many ways: through journal writing, sharing sessions, liturgical training sessions, or retreats. We need to articulate our own stories and listen to the stories of God in those with whom we are building a community. We too easily assume that if we are called as parishioners or staff to ministry that it is the same Lord who is calling us and that the good will we have toward another is adequate grounding for smooth working relationships. Nothing could be further from the truth. Each of us has a different God—shaped by our interaction with a particular place in a particular family, in a particular neighborhood. School, work, finances, marriage, singleness, and celibacy fashion our peculiar relationship with the Lord. Through these encounters we have unique understandings of sin, grace, faith, hope, and love that set us apart from others who have not walked our path. Religious words will have different meanings because we have had different experiences.

As we listen to each other we understand the background music of the words and begin to create a symphony of praise, which is the liturgy, out of this rich variety of experiences. It is through these experiences of sharing our struggles, our joys, and our hopes that we can be comfortable in praying with one another. In our haste to hurry through an agenda we pass each other's spaceships in the atmosphere. If we know each other only through the books we have read and tapes we have listened to, we can understand why our liturgies seem contrived or wooden. They are expressions of our heads rather than of our hearts.

The chief tool of a professional or nonprofessional counselor is self-knowledge. The professional's training is never separated from self-discovery, coming to know one's self. As the counselor comes to terms with her life and sees it as her own, and therefore limited, the temptation to use it as a model or reference point as she listens to another is diminished. The liturgical ministers of a parish can be flawed by thinking that their way is better because of ordination, education, or a call to ministry. We have a built-in condition of subtly conveying to people that our way is better. If liturgical ministers learn to listen to each other, they can begin to listen to the assembly and to respect its understanding of worship, thus seeing themselves as resources and enablers rather than dictators.

Contemplation and Action

In the history of Christian spirituality we have always had a tension between the poles of contemplation and action. Unless contemplation leads to action, it is sterile. Unless activism is rooted in contemplation, it will become harsh and strident. While one hand washes the other, we have different understandings of how they are put together, which in turn is reflected in the liturgical style of assemblies. We may presume that the people at seven o'clock Sunday Mass come because they prefer a quiet Mass that would be more inclined to a contemplative approach, which includes periods of silence plus readings, preaching, and prayers in a subdued voice that does not interfere with their desire to focus inwardly. The people who come to later Masses may find the Spirit in touching, singing, readings, and preaching that resound and vibrate, mingled with audible joy and laughter. In any scholarly presentation of the history of Christian spirituality both contemplation and action would be affirmed as essential ingredients of an authentic Christian spirituality, along with respect for both inner space and expressions of affectivity.

Liturgy as Mystery

The White Robed Monk[3] is an Ira Progoff meditation that illustrates a contemplative stance toward community or assemblies. The meditation begins by drawing us into a

quiet place within ourselves. The process is called centering. After one has this awareness of being present to oneself, one sees through fantasy a tree stump with many
circles, rooting us in our history. The tree stump becomes
for us an altar. Next there is an awareness that there are
others in the room. They are monks deep in prayer. Each is
into the depths of his own well. One becomes conscious that
each of the monks, while into his own prayer, is aware that
each is drawing at the same time from the same source.
There is deep communion in the silence.

While doing a Progoff meditation one can feel the
energies throughout the room even though one does not
know the names of other registrants or their feelings about
the workshop. Each experiences the entire group as people
together in a communal prayer event. The guided meditation created a contemplative assembly. This is what Keifer
calls the spirituality of mystery.

> It is an intense intuition of there being something
> elusive, haunting, indirect, yet utterly compelling
> about which life relentlessly revolves. There is a sense
> of being drawn or pursued by something that is never
> quite tangible, that never quite allows any sense of a
> face to face meeting. It is more of a force, an elusive
> something, unnameable, and inscrutable, yet demand-
> ing the full attention of my person . . . . This is
> perhaps the reason why many otherwise not so con-
> servative young people will prefer an antique form of
> ritual: it offers a means of expressing a spirituality of
> mystery which many gesturally impoverished con-
> temporary liturgies do not.[4]

Touching the Lord

People whose spirituality is rooted in relationships find
mystery or the sacred evoked in human interaction. It is
what Sam Keen in *To a Dancing God* describes as visceral
theology.

> A visceral theology majors in a sense of *touch* rather
> than a sense of *hearing*. That our age is post-

Reformation means that it no longer hears the word of God with the ear of faith. The sacred must be redis- covered in what moves and touches us, in what makes us tremble, in what is proximate rather than remote, ordinary rather than extraordinary, native rather than imported. . . . without denying the urgent need for a more playful use of language, particularly theological language, we must insist that words alone, even poetic words are not enough. It is the real, literal carnal body that must be resensitized and educated in the sacred- ness which lies hidden in its feelings.[5]

A quiet liturgy for the First Friday assembly at Calumet City's Country Manor Nursing Home would be a disaster without the tactile. The attention span of most residents is minimal. Aural and verbal faculties have seri- ously deteriorated. It is the visual, sound, and touch that can carry the liturgy, but of these three it is the tactile or carnal that has the greatest possibility of mediating the sacred. Since the purpose of the tactile in the liturgy is not to create or establish social relationships with worshipers, it can easily be subverted into cheap and banal friendliness. The visceral or carnal needs to be severely disciplined in the liturgy to lead us to the sacred.

Beyond the Emotional

According to Charles Davis, liturgy

is a dramatic action and a dramatic action requires care in the way it is done. It requires that nothing be done to destroy a kind of tension of the celebration. There is nothing more wearisome, more destructive both of prayer and of the creation of a community than a kind of artificial friendliness and informality. A genuine liturgy should have an objectivity which remains inde- pendent of the varying moods of participants, so that one can take part in it at a time when one's actual emotional responses may be below that of the liturgy but not the tension.

The liturgy as a celebration should not be dependent upon an immediacy of response. Otherwise it creates hypocrisy and a wrong kind of tension. It is a violation of personal integrity and feeling. When one is expected to make an immediate and direct response of a certain kind, this is to do violence. What one should have is a celebration that mediates differences of feelings and states of minds of different people at different times. If you want an immediacy of response, you don't want the liturgy. You should simply have an informal get-together.[6]

In the sixties we suddenly switched from a liturgical style that did not allow for feelings and self-expression to one that allowed for creativeness. The result of a decade of floundering around trying to see what worked was a loss of reverence, our pearl of great price. This book, liturgy workshops, and conventions are aids helping us discover ways of ritualizing that are prayerful, human, and faithful to our tradition in an effort to recover a lost reverence or sacredness. Our primitive instincts tell us that a loss of reverence leads to a loss of faith.

While Davis pleads for objectivity and Keifer for reverencing the mystery, charismatic spirituality has emphasized the spontaneous. It does not root its spirituality or assemblies in a tightly structured ritual or contemplative silence but in storytelling and spontaneous prayer. Those who have a need to verbalize their feelings about themselves, others, and the world and how the Spirit is at work in their lives find that charismatic assemblies meet these needs with an authentic way of touching the sacred in life. While it may seem to purists to be a reification of the Spirit, a vulgarization of mystery, for others it is an authentic way of talking about and relating to the inscrutable, unknowable presence of God and the mystery of salvation.

Spirituality deals with human hungers: the hunger for space to enter a contemplative state, the hunger to be present to and even touch other humans, the hunger to share our joys and sorrows in song, poetry, and prose, the hunger to articulate our alienation, the hunger to cry out or act out a prophetic rage. While a liturgical assembly is not an adequate forum for addressing all these hungers, they exist, however muted, in every assembly. It is the assembly that can respond to the dominant hungers without being swallowed by them. Since liturgical assemblies draw their power from a tradition that has for centuries developed rituals for addressing themselves to these hungers, we cannot deviate too far from the tradition or ritual without losing its power to facilitate our spiritual development.

Questions for Reflection and Discussion

1. Who is God for me? How have I experienced God's presence in the history of my life? When have I experienced God's mercy and forgiveness? What is my image of God right now in my life? Has it changed from when I was a child? an adolescent?

2. Have members of our liturgy team shared with one another their image of God? an experience of God in their life? Would it be beneficial to do so?

3. What does celebrating liturgy do to/for my image of God? my relationship to God?

4. Is my life a balance of contemplation and action? If not, what concrete steps could I take to help this process grow in my life?

5. How is liturgy part mystery? How is God's presence in the world part mystery?

3

SYSTEMS AND STYLES

If each assembly has a life and a spirituality of its own, how can it come to a self-understanding? If the assembly has a self-awareness, it can more fully actualize itself, move more consciously toward what it wants to be, and more effectively reflect its spirituality. The role of the staff person is to facilitate this development, but given the unexamined mindset of our corporate and individual spirituality, it is difficult to imagine how we can even talk about it. Since our spirituality is an unarticulated summation of our relationships with the Lord since childhood, only with great effort can we sort it out apart from the spirituality of a particular assembly. Each is separate and needs to be owned. Without this consciousness the staff person may be subtly manipulating the assembly to make itself into the image and likeness of the dominant staff person. An assembly with some self-awareness of who it is has greater ability to resist manipulation, even if it is simply passive resistance.

There are obvious limitations to an assembly acquiring a self-consciousness. It has no officers, no board of directors, no executive committee, and no plenary session, unless it is the only assembly of the parish. The parish that has a liturgy planning committee for each assembly is an exception. One of the strengths of the Latin American and African basic Christian communities is that each community is autonomous and acts as a committee of the whole.

The Systems Approach

Systems analysis is a rapidly developing branch of communications that helps people grasp what is happening in their family, their work place, the nation, and the infrastructure of the entire world. It is a tool that can be used to understand the dynamics of a particular assembly. Everywhere from worship in which two or three are gathered together in the name of the Lord to multinational corporations there is a system or a pattern for interacting that can be studied. In so doing, one can locate oneself and see how one functions in an environment that has built-in goals, rules, rewards, and punishments which, while never articulated, are not too elusive to identify. It is like a chemical analysis of a glue that holds or fails to hold something together.

Family therapy is built on the discovery that the healing of one member of the family outside of the family unit by personal therapy may have disasterous effects on other members of the family because the sickness of one was "necessary" for the family to function. The child no longer misbehaving may be the occasion for the parents to get a divorce because they were held together by the deviant child. The alcoholic parent who suddenly stops drinking may drive others to drink or to behave in bizarre ways because the scapegoat necessary for family functioning has been removed. The family therapist, rather than try to save one member from the clutches of the family system, works with all the relationships of the entire family at the same time to help the family function more effectively as a system that gives support and nourishment to all. The task is not necessarily to change the system, although this might happen, but for each to understand how the entire system is working. In the process each becomes freed from the oppressiveness of the system without leaving.

One of the discoveries of people who take part in a systems analysis of a particular situation is the awareness that each person has influence. Passive aggression through silence, fidgetiness, mock laughter, or looking at one's watch are ways we covertly use this influence to undermine the effectiveness of the "take over" personality. When we begin to see our own complicity in the situation, we begin to take responsibility for our behavior and see the system change. When we have a grasp of a systems approach to an assembly or other gathering we take a more creative stance toward helping the system to function in the way that the group desires.

In a liturgical assembly we begin to identify our behavior patterns and those of others as they relate within the assembly. A presider may be a hail-fellow-well-met until he puts on the robes and changes the cheerful smile to the solemn mien that he thinks the assembly expects of him. Eucharistic ministers, ushers, readers, and servers could take on this solemn posturing because they see it in the presider who sees it in them. The circle is closed; the double bind is in place. The liturgy becomes a sorrowful assembly which is dedicated to making everyone look unhappy. The circle is broken when people are willing to test out other behaviors to see if, indeed, this is who people are and what they really want.

Looking at the assembly as a system helps us to relate to the assembly and challenges us not to name too easily the spirituality of others. All of us need a listening ear and an understanding heart to know what we and others think and believe. "How do I know what I think until I hear myself talk?" captures the wisdom of the ages.

Parish Styles

A vantage point to assess whether the spirituality of an assembly indeed is reflected in the liturgy is the church parking lot before and after the assembly. The relaxed or hurried look, the body movements, the casual remarks or grim silence tell us whether or not participants are marching to the tune of the assembly drummer. If they are not relaxed and smiling, it may mean that they should march to another drummer or that the drummer should drum to their beat.

In spite of what we are writing on the autonomy of the parish assembly, the hard-nosed reality is that this autonomy is circumscribed by several levels of authority outside the assembly, namely, the liturgical committee, the parish council, the pastor, the associate pastor, visiting clergy, diocesan regulations, decrees from the Vatican congregation, and the admonitions and style of liturgy of the pope.

Although the pastor may feel his authority has eroded since collegiality was mandated as the official style of church leadership, his attitude toward liturgy has the most pervasive single influence, whether his permissiveness or active involvement is felt by the liturgical committee and other presiders. A second factor is how diocesan and Roman decrees are interpreted. If the bishop and pastor reinforce each other in maintaining the authoritarian structure of pre-Vatican II, there is little opening for a particular assembly to begin to see itself as a group that has even a very limited or circumscribed authority. This indeed may be the authentic spirituality of some assemblies and, like the plea of a few for a Latin Mass, it must be respected.

Adventures of a Collegial Parish[1] is the story of Father Robert Fuller, appointed to form a new parish in a developing, affluent area of Tuscon, Arizona. Although without the experience of having been an associate pastor, he was intellectually committed to collegiality as a style of leadership. A staff and core of volunteers accepted his vision and quickly put in place a collegial parish. After the honeymoon, parishioners with different spiritualities who felt forced into a corner demanded accountability in a parish meeting called Black Sunday. After the blood was mopped from the sanctuary and some parishioners left because they found there was no spiritual home for them at St. Pius, the community at a painfully high price became a parish with a distinct view of church and a greater sensitivity to minority understandings. The ownership and collegiality moved from the staff and core parishioners to the entire parish through the Red Sea after the experience of Black Sunday.

Many pastors neurotically look over their shoulders to see if a diocesan or Vatican official is taking notes for a purge. It is a device the pastor may be using as an excuse for not allowing the assemblies and the parish to achieve a greater level of autonomy. Father John Maxwell, pastor of St. Andrew's in Oakland, does not fit this category. He writes in *Worship in Action:*

> Following the insight of Vatican II which freed the Church from the rigid uniformity mandated since the Council of Trent, we believe that "liturgy is for the people," not that "the people are for the liturgy." We see great value in the reformed Roman rite and the

expanded lectionary. However, we feel that this is only a starting point and not an end in itself. St. Andrew's tries to adapt the worship service to accommodate the present real needs of our West Oakland inner-city community. If we are to speak to the real-life situations of our people, then we must have the freedom to experiment and develop a local religious experience of faith. Our ideal is to remain true to the great liturgical tradition of past Christian ages and, at the same time, to speak to the human and spiritual needs of a unique people at a unique point of time in a unique cultural and geographic situation. While we ratify and glory in this uniqueness, we try to see the universality of our human and religious encounter. We want to emphasize the fact that we are tied inseparably to all other peoples on this planet and our roots extend to all of the past.

This openness to change means that we are always evolving, growing, and becoming. . . . A scriptural reading that was relevant for last week's funeral may not be appropriate for the burial of a man who died of a heroin overdose a week later.

We do not favor change for change's sake. We really try to resist the frenetic and sometimes endless chase for novelty. Working very hard to be sensitive to the needs of our community, we utilize all aids to worship, both the tried and true and the innovative."[2]

Assemblies are often given birth and incubated by a liturgical committee or a religious education committee of parents who claim their own authority and feel free to be innovative. The Moppet Mass could only exist in a parish like St. Mary's in Colts Neck, N. J., with a pastor like Father William Bausch. This is described in *The Christian Parish*.[3]

This can happen only in a parish in which the pastor is not simply permissive but liturgically intelligent and secure about his own personhood.

When the system is tightly locked by pastors and others who police the parish for deviation, then the parishioner must frankly face the question of membership and ask about changing parish affiliation. If its members have no access to shaping the assembly, one may owe it to oneself and family to budget a few more miles of gas for Sunday worship. While the geographical boundaries of parishes in the American Catholic church have been a stroke of ecclesiastical genius, they are not sacred cows.

The spirituality of each parishioner is influenced by the dominant spirituality of the parish or assembly, and the dominant spirituality of the parish is in turn influenced by the spirituality of each parishioner. When we begin to identify the spirituality of our parish assembly, we can become more comfortable with the points of departure from our own. When we understand the forces that have fed and continue to feed its corporate spirituality, we become more tolerant of its failure to meet all of our needs. Compassion grows from the grace of accepting what cannot be changed.

Questions for Reflection and Discussion

1. What is the spirituality of the people at each of our parish Masses?

2. Does the liturgy flow from their spirituality?

3. Does the liturgy call them to growth rather than stagnation?

4

LEADERSHIP IN THE ASSEMBLY

Every assembly has appointed ministers: presiders, homilists, lectors, servers, musicians, eucharistic ministers. If the assembly is to become itself, the ideal is for ministers to come out of the assembly. At this stage in history the presider is the obvious exception. He is an ordained, professional, celibate minister from outside the assembly. If the parish has many assemblies and many presiders, it may try to fit the spirituality of the priest to the spirituality of the assembly. The retired pastor may be best able to relate to assemblies of retired people. However, we may find a young priest came from the seminary with built-in rigidities lacking the flexibility to relate to assemblies of older people as easily as some elderly priests who can relate easily with assemblies of young and old. In many parishes a rotation of presiders is preferred so that assemblies do not become cut off from the total parish by relating each week to only one of the weekend presiders. Other leadership roles in the assembly, with the possible exception of the ministers of music, are best taken from the assembly of which they are a part.

Since the assembly does not have a discerning process for the selection of its ministers, a staff member is usually assigned to facilitating the assembly, discovering the gifted, and calling them forth. In a very small assembly at a morning Mass or a rural mission outpost there may be a member of the assembly who is acknowledged to have the charisma for discerning and calling forth people who are extremely modest and unaware of their giftedness.

Where Do Ministers Come From?

Ideally, liturgical ministers should come from the assembly they most frequently belong to or feel part of. The need for lectors, eucharistic ministers, liturgy team members, ushers, and others should be first brought to the assembly itself so that those with the particular gifts needed for that ministry will surface. Certainly, the sharing of needs can also take place through bulletin articles, commentator announcements, and effective Sunday homilies.

The approach that seems to be most successful is the support/encouragement model in which personal contact is the key. People in the assembly can see themselves as enablers of one another and claim as their responsibility the calling forth of people from among their own number to serve in specific ministries. This certainly is quite different from the "will anybody help Father out?" approach that permeated so much of our initial choosing of ministers. The people themselves need a heightened awareness of the gifts among them and encouragement from one another to share them in a larger ritual context.

We are inviting the assembly to look at the humanity of each person in the community, to look at their strengths and weaknesses, to look at their roles in everyday life. Those who speak for a living, such as salespeople, shopkeepers, and teachers, might like to extend their life's work in service of their worshiping community as lectors. Those who have a quiet, personal style, who relate well in one-to-one situations, and who can look people in the eye in a way that conveys openness and not judgment can be invited to extend their life's attitude and gifts to service of the community as eucharistic ministers. Those who appreciate, enjoy, and delight in music, from young to old, can be asked to help others in their worshiping community to share their joy by serving as a minister of music.

To know these lifestyles, gifts, and talents, the assembly needs to know or have familiarity with one another. While in the context of the eucharist, I may or may not speak directly to Mr. Laurents, but I know him through my family, through my neighborhood, and through his work with the park district boys' basketball team. I may also be aware of his orderliness, his posture, and his reverence for the holy without ever talking to him, simply by observing the way he prays at liturgy. Perhaps this is a person who might like to serve the need of his celebrating community as a trainer of altar servers. I might stop him after Mass for a few minutes to share my insights with him—to ask him to consider this important ministry, but also to support and encourage him by telling him why I think he might be just the person we need. I also would add that the pastoral staff of the parish has said that it is willing to give ongoing assistance to the person who would take over this ministry and that they would do the initial training with him.

Training Programs

Although the personal approach may fit a small or rural parish like Ford City, St. Victor with 5,000 plus weekly worshippers needs an alternate approach, a more democratic and structured way of calling forth members of the assembly. An appeal in the Sunday bulletin for recruits for a particular ministry is a simple method. Many parishes have "Commitment Sunday," in which people are given an opportunity to indicate their willingness to serve on committees, perform specific tasks, or sign up for a liturgical ministry. The strength of this method is in opening up the process of selection to the entire parish. The weakness is in attracting people who have no obvious competency. We can combine these approaches by encouraging people we feel gifted for a particular ministry, but with the understanding that there will be a discernment process. An interview with each person volunteering for a ministry is a helpful screening device. The training program itself will offer the trainer and the trainee an opportunity to discuss competency or lack of it, in which case an alternate ministry can be discussed.

During the training sessions we make it clear that people are training for a ministry in a particular assembly. Since people must arrange their lives to include family responsibilities that take them away from the assembly to which they normally belong, we need an adequate back-up list to allow for people not being available a third of the Sundays of the year. When we insist on ministers coming out of particular assemblies, the only ones rotating all assemblies will be the presiders and the organist, which roles are limited by ordination and technical musical competency.

It is not enough to accept volunteers. Besides a training program we need an effective support system. We do not expect people to put themselves and their self-esteem on the line without being brother and sister to them in season and out of season. Parishes that have recruited lectors, given them one training session in which only movement patterns were discussed, and then scheduled them and handed them a missalette to practice from, have had disastrous effects. It is no wonder that within a year the parish was again looking for a large number of new lectors.

There are parishes in the United States that began introducing communion from the cup at Sunday Masses, but failed to meet with their eucharistic ministers to talk about it, to practice it, or even to get their consent for it. It is no wonder that on the first Sunday when the practice was introduced, both assembly and ministers wanted to drop the practice immediately. All were uncomfortable because the assembly had not been catechized as to the reasons and the manner of practice itself and the ministers hadn't been sufficiently trained in this new function.

Ministry in the liturgical assembly is not, at the beginning, an easy or comfortable service for the minister or for

the assembly. It takes time, patience, and practice for growth to take place. We open up ourselves to a new experience, we struggle with what it does to our old notions, and if we can break through, we find new insight and new meaning into the mystery of life, the mystery of Jesus. This struggle and growth process is not signifcantly different in a specified minister or a member of the assembled ministering community.

Limitations of Liturgical Ministries

In recent years there has been a heavy accent on preparing people for fulltime ministry. Some become fulltime lay or religious staff members, others become deacons or publicly commissioned ministers who have been certified for a particular ministry. Seminaries, secular divinity schools, and some Catholic university pastoral theology departments offer programs that lead to professional degrees in ministry. Others are ordained deacons, which in itself does not qualify one for a particular ministry, but does put the church "Good Housekeeping Seal of Approval" on one as a public minister.

Judy Pilarski does not fit any of the above. She chides her colleagues and friends about referring to her as a minister or being a part of a ministry committee simply because she belongs to the banner committee. She enjoys the one morning a week with the women as they design, cut, sew, and use the multiple skills of the group. To the staff she may be a minister but she rejects such a title and prefers to be an unacclaimed volunteer. She does not want to be imprisoned by a new name for churchy people.

This reaction to ministry is scored both here and abroad. The Chicago Declaration states:

> It is our experience that a wholesome and significant movement within the church—the involvement of lay people in many church ministries—has led to a devaluation of the unique ministry of lay men and women. The tendency has been to see lay ministry as involvement in some church-related activity, for example, religious education, pastoral care for sick and elderly or readers in church on Sunday.[1]

From England, Mark Gibbs writes:

> Some great Protestant parishes not only offer their members fine opportunities for worship and for Christian learning, they almost imprison the laity in a ceaseless round of churchly activities as if, in Harvey Cox's phrase, Christian soldiers may expect to gain medals by staying in the barracks. Can your Catholic parishes equip your laity without entrapping them in church structures? Can they learn to be the people of God in the world as well as at Mass?[2]

In this book, training for liturgical ministries is not seen as a training for ministry in a total sense. It is built on helping people to serve more effectively a particular assembly. We are interested in people acquiring skills for a particular situation rather than certifying them as ministers for the diocese or even the entire parish. The ideal is to offer the skills training locally, not having people withdraw from the community to become special people or to limit their time for their contribution to secular community. The goal is to keep the ministers rooted in the assembly which is in turn rooted in a wider church and culture.

Questions for Reflection and Discussion

1. How do we call forth liturgical ministers from our parish? Does the way we call them forth reflect ministry rooted in baptism or "helping Father out"?

2. How do we train our liturgical ministers? Is this sufficient? Is it ongoing? Does it allow for reflection on spirituality as well as ministry?

3. How do we prepare our assemblies for new ministries or changes in ministry?

5

LITURGICAL PLANNING

Liturgy planning committees did not exist a decade ago. When Mass was the priest's preserve, he assumed full responsibility for its execution; it was Father Jones' Mass. In the parishes which have moved toward the liturgy as an assembly that celebrates as a community rather than as spectators at the celebration of Father's Mass, ownership for shaping the liturgy is claimed by the body. The shaping must be done by a representative group that orchestrates the event in a way that brings all its parts together in a symphony. The priest may do well in his role as presider, but he may lack the leadership gifts, the time, or the desire to be the coordinator. A liturgical planning committee assumes the responsibility for particular liturgies, for the entire liturgical services of the parish, or for some agreed-upon segments.

Ford City Catholic Center in Chicago began as an experimental parish in a shopping center. It came on the scene as the avant-garde were trying to appropriate the theology of Vatican II that sees the parish Sunday liturgy as the celebration of the entire assembly. Thirteen years ago when the pastoral staff began its work of nurturing community, liturgy planning meetings played a significant role. Each Tuesday evening the pastoral staff would gather with community members to reflect on the scripture for the upcoming weekend. These meetings were open to all, with invitations being extended in the bulletin, by announcement, and most importantly by personal invitation. The meeting would begin with prayer followed by proclamation of the weekend's scripture passages. Then the staff would share and invite others to share their reflections on the scripture passages, or how they saw them enfleshed in their own lives.

At first, the community members present looked to the priests for the correct interpretation of the scriptures and for historical background. But once that was accomplished, and as various people began to know, and trust themselves to one another, sharing would take place at a deeper level. The proclamation and interiorization of the word would lead to prayerful reflection, which might in turn lead to conversion or action. One of the significant aspects of the liturgy planning meetings, besides that of deep faith-sharing, was that the homily was formed right at the meeting. That is, the homilist for the upcoming weekend would take notes as the discussion progressed and those notes would become the basis for the homily. The reflections, the thoughts, the faith-sharing, and the strength of each person was affirmed as they saw themselves significantly contributing to the development of the Sunday celebration. They witnessed their own lives taking on deeper meaning as they listened to the homily on the following weekend, for the homilist spoke not only to them, but about them and with them.

But that was not the end of liturgy meetings. Once notes for the homily were taken, prayers formed, and music chosen, the staff and community present shared a meal. Whether it was coffee and cake, cheese and crackers, homemade pizza, or diet pop and potato chips, almost everyone stayed well over the close of the formal part of the meeting to learn about others, about their families, friends, jobs, common interests, common visions, and past parish experiences. Much of the conversation would flow directly from the sharing that took place at the meeting itself. No one was forced into speaking either during the meeting or afterwards, and yet when each was ready, the invitation was always present to share a part of themselves with the community and to be accepted as who they were.

As liturgy planning meetings continued and knowledge of liturgical principles increased in the community, a time came for the staff and community to face some important realities. The liturgy of each Sunday is part of a liturgical year and that year has cycles. While each weekend liturgy seemed to be effective in itself at the Center, it was seldom that the liturgies together formed into liturgical seasons. The community was not being led through the rhythms of the Christian liturgical year. It was from these feelings and futile attempts to try to combine seasonal planning with weekly faith-sharing meetings that the liturgy team evolved. The liturgy team was formed of community and staff members who were interested in delving deeper into the eucharistic liturgy and into the seasons that our church celebrates throughout the year. Membership was open to anyone with those interests.

The beginnings of the Ford City meetings reminded me of a liturgy planning meeting I attended as a guest at St. Andrew's parish in West Oakland, California. It began with frivolity before dinner; laughter became interlaced with serious discussion during the meal. The agenda was to put a Sunday liturgy together. In alternate moods of light-heartedness and seriousness through rambling digressions which everybody seemed to enjoy, the liturgy somehow came together. The planning meeting was like a St. Andrew's Sunday liturgy: a joyful, homespun celebration of people who liked being with each other, and beneath it all in some subliminal way one experienced the risen Christ, the paschal mystery.

The early planning sessions of Ford City and St. Andrew's weekly meetings are probably more like the New Testament liturgies than their weekend eucharistic liturgies. There is the joyful gathering, the breaking of the bread, the reading and discussion of the scriptures and the intense and joyfilled fellowship of people who have experienced the Lord. Each group would try to recapture on the weekend what they had experienced at the meeting. In both cases it was closer to a noneucharistic liturgy (*koinonia*) or fellowship than a typical liturgy planning committee meeting.

Both parishes, while atypical, offer a model for beginners. Committee members need to experience the Lord being present to them in the noneucharistic committee assembly before they can plan liturgies that offer to larger numbers the possibility of experiencing the Lord as they did in these fellowship meetings. Since the purpose of a liturgical planning committee is to help a parish to experience communal prayer, the group itself should first have experienced it when they gather to plan parish prayer events.

Since we can hardly expect members of the parish who have commitments to a family or a demanding job to give themselves to an all-consuming evening a week, we must scale down our objectives. The first question that must be answered is, "Why a Planning Committee?" Many pastors ask this question. First, it was mandated by Vatican II that the faithful, the members of the celebrating assembly, should take part as much as possible in the planning of the liturgy. Second, and more important, the ritual is a script. Each Sunday the script dramatizes a facet of the story that is told through actors who use words, song, art, and dramatic action. If the story is to be dramatized well, it needs to be understood in its parts and as a whole, coordinated and rehearsed. The ritual or script has to be digested thoroughly by the director and actors. The script for a particular Sunday must be understood and interpreted in its relationship to the entire yearly cycle, which dramatizes the paschal mystery in its parts and as a whole.

Although the evidence seems to be in favor of such a committee, the question must still be asked: Do we want an overall parish liturgical planning commission? The answer can come only from a discussion of the staff and parish council. Without the enthusiastic support of the staff and council, it would be an exercise in futility for any staff member to accept the commission to form such a group. The staff may be working out of a pre-Vatican II theology that sees the role of the people in the pews as pray-ers, payers, and obeyers and the celebrant as adequate to direct the liturgy without a detailed script and rehearsals. Wisdom might dictate that we have the patience of the man in the gospel who waited thirty-eight years for someone to lift him into the pool when the Spirit moved the waters.

If indeed the staff and parish elders agree that there is a need for an overall planning committee, the starting point could be a task force that limits itself to specific and limited objectives. This would be seen as repair work, making immediate changes in music, lectors, or whatever, but not touching the foundations. The other model would be to develop a committee that sees itself as an overall advisory committee, which could speak to the totality of parish worship. It would see itself not as a task force but as an enduring parish structure that would continue after the initial members have served and moved on.

The Liturgist

According to the *Official Catholic Directory*, Ford City Catholic Center Parish has a staff of one, the ordained priest. According to the Ford City parish community there are six co-equal pastors: a priest, a lay person, a sister, and three permanent deacons. As co-pastors, each shares in the liturgical, teaching, and caring ministries. Although all of them have liturgical roles, only one of them is *the* liturgist, the one in charge of the overall liturgical planning and execution, the one who is liaison with the liturgical planning team, the presider, the homilists, the musicians, the art and environment team, the lectors, the eucharistic ministers, and the framers of these various ministries. Our present tradition assigns this role to the ordained pastor or youngest associate.

At Ford City the liturgist is the lay co-pastor, the co-author of this book. It is her training in drama and music plus her decade of experience working with the planning team, her theological studies, and her work with the Archdiocesan Office for Divine Worship and Liturgy Training Publications that has prepared her for this role.

The Ford City model shatters the old way of thinking that a theological education and ordination automatically qualify the priest to be *the* liturgist. It denies that the person who relates to the liturgical planning team, the liturgical art and environment committee, and the musicians as a coor-

dinator, must be a priest. The person who has the professional liturgical training that empowers him or her to relate to and see the parts as a whole should ideally be an artist with a theological background in liturgy. Obviously such people are rare, but the statement offers a guideline for us to approximate.

It could be destructive to a priest who is gifted as an administrator, social activist, teacher, or counselor to be saddled with the liturgical leadership role in an area in which he has no special gifts other than to be a warm and loving presider who can act out the script given him by the planning team. It is the distinction we make in sports between coach and players and in theater between scriptwriter, director, and actor.

The Ford City model underscores the liturgist as a full time co-pastor as distinguished from an expert who is hired by the parish to perform a single function. The liturgist is not a staff appendage who adds an aesthetic dimension to liturgy, but a core person who teaches and does the pastoral care tasks as do the other core staff members. The radical difference from other models is that the lay liturgist is a co-pastor. It is not a hierarchical model that leaves the final decision to one person, but a model that is congruent with our theology of the assembly.

The staff liturgist catches the flow of all the parts—presiders, preachers, musicians, artists, lectors, and other ministers—as well as the flow that comes from the community through its ethnic or social mix, and from the assembly that expresses itself in prayer the way it does. The staff liturgist is the liaison with the variety of liturgical ministries and committees. The size of, and the personality of, the liturgies, the parish, or the liturgical assembly will determine the specifics of how she or he acts as a channel that keeps a circular flow. In preparing seasons, such as Advent/Christmastime and Lent/Eastertime, the liturgist may want to meet with representative members of each of these groups. It takes genius to have everyone in communication with each other without adding another meeting.

Each liturgy can be seen as a drama in which every element of the ritual must be pondered and fleshed out in the liturgist's mind before it can be executed by the ministers. Just as the director of a play has to create a living, vibrant experience from the written word and a few stage directions, the liturgist is responsible for bringing life to the word and the directives of the liturgical books.

The liturgist is to create a living prayer experience out of scripture and rubrics—a written text. Goals include being faithful to the text and the season, recognizing the cause for celebration that our church is calling us to in a particular liturgy, and achieving the best prayer experience possible for the assembly by striving for excellence rather than settling for mediocrity.

The liturgist needs extensive knowledge of the liturgical documents, sign and symbol, ritual, the liturgical year, and the ministries of the liturgy. The liturgist must be a person of prayer, able to work well with the various ministers and artists who are integral to the liturgical action.

The liturgist is responsible for the complete liturgy and therefore has much work to do before the liturgy ever begins. First, the rite itself must be studied for a thorough understanding of the important elements, the ritual action called for, and the shape of the rite. Second, by being enmeshed in the season in which the rite is being celebrated, the liturgist can ensure that the rite flows into and out of the liturgical year. A third requirement is an awareness of the strengths and weaknesses of the ministers who will help to celebrate the rite with the assembly. Finally, the liturgist must take into serious account the assembly in which the celebration is taking place—its ethnic and political character and the degree of its openness to experience in many and various ways the presence of God in an assembly of faith.

While the pastor or associate is the authorized person to oversee the liturgical life of the parish, he plays his role best when he remains an overseer and a possible resource person rather than a director and *factotum*. He needs to trust the liturgist and liturgical planners to grow through experience, through successes and failures, and through continued education. Whether or not he is an active member of the planning committee, his presence will be felt. He is the key to the limits to which the planners can go in their creativeness and style. His theology, liturgical sense, and flexibility will be one of the parameters of the group.

Diversity of Roles

While this book offers no hints on the recycling of priests, it does suggest that one would not become a planner unless one is capable of handling a high level of frustration. The other limit of creativeness will be the committee itself. The committee needs a membership that reflects the wide cultural and educational levels of the community, people with an appreciation of the arts as well as people who are close to the street, to offer feedback. It needs prayerful, reflective people and ideally a few people who are willing to read the liturgical documents for the group. We are searching for baptized believers who have a commitment to communal public prayer.

If liturgy is to have an honest feeling about it, it must come from the people who pray it. Saint and sinner, musician and usher, grandmother and teenager—all should have the opportunity to affect the prayer of the assembly to which they belong. Certainly a few facilitating and skilled roles are needed, for example, a coordinator to orchestrate the meetings and keep the lines of communication open and clear. A musician and artist are needed as resources. If we are preparing a particular liturgy, the homilist's listening presence would be a way that God's saving word, found in the weekend's scriptures, would enter into his being and flow back to the assembly through his openness to the lives of the liturgical committee, which ideally is representative of the assembly.

Ongoing Education and Formation

Liturgical planners map out the direction or theme the liturgy takes for the seasons and ordinary Sundays and special events. Therefore, liturgical planners need to understand the purpose of liturgy and see it in its yearly cycle, but more important to understand the tradition and why we worship the way we do. A group can get caught in the immediacy of dashing off a liturgy script for the next Sunday or of putting out fires when it needs to spend time on the overall thrust of parish worship.

The failure to take the long-range approach is endemic to all of us, as Archbishop Rembert Weakland confesses.[1]

> I feel one of our greatest obstacles is that we have not been able to really plan a consistent liturgical renewal. I feel indeed guilty, as chairman of the Bishops' Committee on the Liturgy, that I too have not been able to think out the kind of planning that is needed at this moment. It seems to be that we go from one crisis situation to another and cannot work in that scientific and reflective way that is needed for careful planning. Perhaps many of the other obstacles listed also impinge on our desire, even our willingness to face a long-term commitment.

It might be well for the committee to take an extended period, even a year, to come to know each other, to work and pray together, to agree on who they are as a committee, and to set limits for themselves. They have a need to discover themselves as a community of faith as did the previously described Ford City and St. Andrew's groups.

During this formation year, a process needs to be adopted as to the direction of these meetings. It is especially crucial to establish this before beginning any planning. Time limits need to be set for each meeting, responsibilities need to be clear, lines of authority or lack of them clearly marked out. Who is ultimately responsible: this group? the liturgy coordinator, the associate, the pastor? Can Father Visitor come in one weekend and change the whole liturgy to suit himself? Answers to these questions will combat the terminal disease called beating one's head against the wall.

The year of formation could be telescoped through an all-day workshop. *Goal Setting for Liturgy Committees*[2] is a booklet that guides a committee through this process. It is not an intellectual exercise, but a device to help the group look at themselves, the resources available, the tasks that need to be addressed, and how responsibility is distributed and the work evaluated.

We offer a few suggestions for beginning planners. Start small. Don't begin by planning Christmas or Easter or even the Twenty-Third Sunday in Ordinary Time. Plan a paraliturgy for yourselves. Enter into it fully and criticize it as honestly as possible. Try a communal prayer service for the whole parish, perhaps during Advent or Lent.

When you begin to plan, use the brainstorming technique to talk of images, impressions, feelings, colors, sounds, and smells. The task of providing banners, music, and words can take place later. What frightens you, consoles you, challenges you, surprises you, delights you? The essence of liturgy planning is to let what is truly human come forth. It is in the truly human that we encounter the truly divine. Share your stories in response to word and sacrament.

Models Must Be Adapted

Is the model offered in this chapter applicable to all parishes small, medium, large, and extra large; rural, urban, poor suburb, and affluent suburb; Black, Hispanic, Oriental, and White; North and South? In the diocese of Juneau, Alaska, there is one bishop and ten priests who serve small and widely scattered communities. Not only is the priest's visit infrequent, but because of major snowstorms Sister Immaculate, who travels the diocese, cannot be present every weekend to preside and preach at the paraliturgies of her diocese. The assembly in each town or village acts as a committee of the whole. Through her meetings with these communities she is able to discern who can best lead the paraliturgies each Sunday. In her role of facilitator she helps the assembly become a self-sufficient liturgical assembly without the presence of a priest or sister.

In rural Iowa, Sister Joan Houtekier's task was to be the liturgical resource person for four parishes which had a staff of two priests and two sisters. Her job was to facilitate the development of a liturgical committee in each parish. This pattern is rapidly developing in the Northwest and Southwest. It is becoming obvious that the church will increasingly depend on liturgical committees as the presence of priests diminishes. Without liturgical committees, parishes and the faith they embody may die.

What has been written presents an ideal that may have been developed in a medium-sized, urban parish, but the underlying principles can be applied to the village in Alaska, military bases, and parishes in ethnic and social enclaves. Whether it is two or three gathered in the name of the Lord or two or three thousand in a cathedral, each is an assembly at prayer, which, if it is to be authentic and not a performance, needs to reflect the graced life of the people present. The effectiveness of a committee hinges not on their ability to put together mechanically the parts of a liturgical service, but on their perception of themselves as facilitators for a church assembly engaged in prayer.

Planning for Multiple Assemblies

In the first two chapters we insisted that each assembly was unique in its composition and spirituality. How can a parish liturgical planning committee plan for all the liturgies in the parish? In large urban parishes there may be as many as nine weekend assemblies, plus funerals and marriages. At the Newman parish of the University of Wisconsin, each weekend liturgy is considered an autonomous assembly that has its own liturgical committee. While the strength of this arrangement is obvious, the weakness of several liturgical committees in one parish is the possibility of having several autonomous parishes develop in the one parish.

One of the tasks of a parish liturgical committee would be to address itself to the diversity of assemblies and find ways of each assembly's giving input into its own liturgical expression. The liturgical committee, through bulletin and pulpit announcements, could ask people to come to a coffee and rolls meeting after each Mass, with a member of the commission or a staff member as the facilitator. The agenda could be to get feedback on the music, lectors, homilies, or whatever people might be able to articulate. This information could be made available to the ministers of the particular assemblies and the committee of the whole. After this *ad hoc* listening session a small overseeing committee might be assembled to meet regularly to report to the parish liturgy committee. We are not suggesting that we develop highly organized bureaucratic structures, but there is a need to obtain more detailed feedback than simply, "I liked the service," or "I do not like the hymns."

Liturgical planners are the invisible ministers who put together every detail necessary to create the desired effect. This requires a keen sense of seeing the whole before it is seen in its parts. They will gradually develop a sense of its flow, its patterns of proclamation to response, its actions of high and low intensity. The total dramatic action begins with the planning of how the words, actions, music, and art blend to bring the desired effect. This requires more than sensitivity to the feelings of the congregation. The committee must come to an understanding of church documents and the history of the liturgy, but it would be the better part of wisdom to keep the intellectual content of the task in the background until people have a feel for the task and have achieved some success. Challenges must be tempered to the receptivity of the group at a particular moment, but without challenges the committee will put itself on automatic pilot and find itself out of touch with a church moving through history.

Questions for Reflection and Discussion

1. Is communal prayer an integral part of our liturgy planning meetings? How could we make this a stronger, more intense experience of the presence of God?

2. Is there a person(s) who is the liturgist in our parish? Is such a person needed?

3. Who belongs to the liturgy committee in our parish? Do we have a musician, artist, presider, homilist, liturgist, scripture person, poet (writer), as well as people from the assembly?

4. Have the members of our liturgy committee read the liturgy

documents of Vatican II? Have we discussed them and do we understand their implications for our parish worship?

5. Do we still see each Mass as "Father Smith's Mass," or do we see each Mass as *our* Mass? What is the difference in these two visions? How does each vision alter the way that we plan the liturgies?

6. Has the liturgy team ever planned any other rite except Mass? Why not? Is there an advantage in planning other types of liturgies and prayer services? How does creativity enter into this?

7. Is there a process to our liturgy planning meetings? Does it work well? Does it need to be evaluated, altered, thrown out?

8. How are our liturgies evaluated? Who does the evaluating? How helpful are these evaluations? Does a new process need to be employed?

6

MINISTRY OF MUSIC

When we offer as an opening thought that music is normative for liturgy, we have much explaining to do. In some countries the Catholic faith has been held together for centuries by silent Masses. While Poles and Germans sang as lustily in church as they did in beer gardens and halls, the Irish had to watch for the local constabulary. The Mass was quiet and stealthy. Since the Irish have dominated the American church, through its bishops and priests, music is hardly normative in the American church. The pleas may be stemming from Roman decrees and German liturgists, but morning Masses, weekday and Sunday, do not give one the impression that music is normative. Indeed we might conclude the opposite.

Following the lead of Vatican II the American bishops have made a turn-around. In 1972 the Bishops' Committee on Liturgy wrote:

> Among the many signs and symbols used by the
> Church to celebrate its faith, music is of preeminent

importance. As sacred song united to the words it forms an integral part of solemn liturgy. Yet the function of music is ministerial; it must serve and never dominate. Music should assist the assembled believers to express and share the gift of faith that is within them and to nourish and strengthen their interior commitment of faith. It should heighten the texts so that they speak more fully and more effectively. The quality of joy and enthusiasm which music adds to community worship cannot be gained in any other way. It imparts a sense of unity to the congregation and sets the appropriate tone for a particular celebration.[1]

The key word in the text is "celebration." We do not celebrate alone. The assumption is that there is a community gathered to offer praise and thanks for some gift they share with one another. At weekday morning Mass with people scattered in the church, some are plying their beads seeming to use the Mass as a background for "real" prayers. However, the downtown noonday Mass, where people appreciate a priest who will preside prayerfully, respond to the readings briefly, and be finished in slightly under thirty minutes, can be celebrative. Even in this time frame, music can facilitate these goals.

The planning committee's perception of both the assembly and the place of music in worship is crucial. While the church documents since 1962 affirm music as normative, it does not mean that twenty years later the people in the pews have accepted it as their norm for public prayer. The church documents and the literature of liturgists imply a theology and spirituality that have been in the mainstream of Catholic tradition, but it does not mean that this is the dominant theology and spirituality of the assembly.

> Some Christians, accustomed to an older type of piety, find participational worship distracting. Paying attention to other people and relating themselves to a common action prevent them from concentrating on the invisible God they want to worship. But the Christians formed by the Church's renewal do not experience the

attention given to others and the effort to cooperate in gesture and song as something distracting. The divinity they worship is not an entity existing apart from the community; God for them is present in the community as a constitutive element—as its source and deepest dimension. . . . In liturgy the Christian celebrates the divine mystery, present in the community, to whom he relates himself through a multitude of inner acts and outer words and gestures.[2]

Since it is unrealistic to think a people can move from a pietistic, individualistic, novena-type spirituality to a corporate, social spirituality in one or two generations, we must accept this fact as a pastoral challenge, particularly in the ministry of music. To tell people that musical liturgy is normative and mandated by the church is to be insensitive and to perpetuate the authoritarian image of the church. The test of council, papal, episcopal, and parish documents is whether they work. It is the task of the planning committee and the musicians, particularly the director of music, to lead the community from the four-hymn beginnings of the 1950s to the rich variety of music of the eighties. The musicians must be supported by the style of the presiders and other ministers, but especially by the scripturally oriented homilies that illustrate the saving deeds of the Lord being lived out in the community. Without losing the securities of the past the people need to be invited into the new by experiencing the saving word of God in the liturgy and pointing to where it might be found in life.

Imaging God

Each of us has several images of God—a mighty wind, an earthquake, a fire, a gentle breeze, a rock, a father embracing a lost son, Jacob wrestling with the angel. Our images, which come out of our life experiences, may vacillate between a God of wrath and a God of love.

Musicians need to be aware that in a single liturgy we can move through many images of God and many stances toward life. We can revert to the child's dependency on parents, become the adult who is capable of decisions and willing to take responsibility for the world, and revert again to the needy child before the closing hymn. While people may want the liturgy to support their flight from reality and endorse their passivity in the face of their self-deception, the liturgy with its style of music and choice of responses and hymns must call people gently and forcefully to face the ambiguities of life and the insecurity of the pilgrim.

If we as a staff, parish council, or liturgy planning team accept musical liturgy as normative for public prayer, the orientation of the parish and of worship in particular will be making a significant shift. The parish will be choosing one value over another, which will ultimately be reflected in the parish's major theological statement, the annual budget. When the assembly of an Alaskan village decides that its assemblies will be musical liturgies, it will generate an assessment of its resources.

The first decision may be to get a hymnal from which

James L. Shaffer

the group can make selections of familiar hymns, or it may be simply for someone to order a cassette of scripturally based songs by the St. Louis Jesuits. If it is a cathedral or large affluent parish, the first task will be the process for setting up a task force from the liturgy team to prepare a job description for a professional director of music. Between the tiny assembly and the large well-heeled parish, there will be a variety of strategies for initiating the process that will reflect the values of a parish which gives a high priority to musical liturgy.

Hard Facts

The pastoral theological question is: What percentage of our parish budget will be apportioned to developing a musical liturgy? The decision makers may need time to be convinced. Compromises can be made by alloting a limited sum for the coming year with the understanding that there will be substantial increments each year as the joyous worshippers dig deeper into their pockets and purses to finance a program that serves the entire congregation Sunday after Sunday rather than at Christmas, Easter, and special events. When music is not a priority and no salary is appropriated for the director, the parish will take whomever has the generosity to be a second class minister satisfied with a Christmas gift and a few patronizing acknowledgments for leading the church choir. As Nathan Mitchell writes:

> In the not-so-distant past musicians in Roman Catholic institutions were regarded, quite simply, as "flunkies." This disparaging image is painfully familiar to persons who have spent long years working in church music. The pastoral musician (we never used that exalted term back then!) was a toady, a green scaly creature who crawled to the organ bench several times a week to play Requiem High Masses, weddings, funerals, and Perpetual Help Novenas. The church musician was regarded as the mediocre talent who couldn't make it in the rough-and-tumble hard-knocks school of pro-

fessional music. Pastoral musicians had no rights, no vote, no recourse, and, naturally, no money. ("You want to be *paid*? I thought you were doing this out of devotion to the church.")[3]

One of the harsh realities of our American culture is the respect or lack of it that is given to a person in proportion to our willingness to invest in the person's office. If the person volunteers his or her services without any gratuity, the parish must insist on paying for fringe expenses as well as making generous allowances for books, supplies, workshops, and professional meetings, which are the normal prerequisite of a professional who is expected to grow. The parish budget committee may also record the contributed services of the professional volunteers as a footnote to the budget.

Musical liturgy as a priority arranges more than line entries on a budget. It says that the director of music is not a second class pastoral assistant but one who is on a par with the presider and the preacher in the formation of the assembly. That directors of music are mostly lay people who have a different understanding of life because of different training and lifestyle may be threatening rather than challenging to priests who in their own understanding of priesthood see themselves as the sole focus for the assembly's spiritual formation. Since the choir directors are the shapers and reflectors of the people's spirituality, they share leadership roles with the presiders and preachers in the development of the corporate prayer life of the community.

As we move away from the pre-Vatican II days when we were happy to have an organist who could just play the chords, we now face not only budgetary priorities but questions about what kind of music ministers we need. The job profile may include coordinators for all the music of the parish and music ministers of particular assemblies. One assembly may respond to a more classical style and another to contemporary. Each needs a minister who can respond with a style of music which is the medium of the assembly's prayer. Since we do not have homogeneous assemblies, we do not want to impose a style that does not express its faith. A larger parish with many assemblies may have a coordinator of music who is able to work with musicians and cantors of particular assemblies.

The Job Description

Ideally the planning team in a large parish would be looking for a music director who has competence in classical and contemporary music and proficiency in guitar, choir, and organ. This is the direction in which professional schools of liturgical music are moving today. Obviously no one director would be able to relate to all of these, but if the parish has a number of communities, the director would at least have a sense of what is good folk, contemporary, or classical music. We repeat, like a choral antiphon running through this book, that the starting place is not what the director's competency is in the abstract but how well she or he relates to specific assemblies and spiritualities of the parish.

If we begin with the axiom that we are what we sing, the spiritual life of the musician comes into focus. The liturgy team must leave to the director the choice of music. The musician will be limited by the repertoire or library that is available. It will be enhanced or inhibited by the musician's spiritual development. If the director is offering the same songs and hymns each year, it might be a sign that neither the director nor the congregation is developing their spirituality through the liturgy. While a congregation may suffer from learning too many new pieces in too short a time, it is a sign of stagnation when a parish does not risk and experiment with new styles and new pieces. If people are singing for a decade "Here We Are All Together" and "Sons of God," it means that the musician has not helped people move spiritually. If we stay with hymns like "A Mighty Fortress Is Our God" without balancing them with loving images of God, it means that our spirituality is not developing with our culture. While we may retain old favorites that cannot have sexist language changed without destroying them, the entire context of our liturgy must be clearly non-sexist.

The director of music needs to have a grasp of the history of liturgy, however minimal; a sense of how the church is moving from a private spirituality that uses liturgy as a background for contemplative prayer or a musical spectacle to a corporate or communal spirituality. A basic minimum would demand an understanding for where we were in the fifties with our four English hymn Masses, which fitted into our three-part Latin Masses, to a liturgy that sees acclamations as the cornerstone of the assembly's response to word and sacrifice. With acclamations at the top of our musical hierarchy, we simply begin with the Memorial Acclamation and Amen. Then we expand to the longer acclamations: the "Holy," responsorial psalm, and the Alleluia verse. The singing during the presentation of the gifts, communion meditation, and recessional hymns are secondary. If this does not represent the spirituality of the assembly, it becomes a challenge to the director and the liturgy team to compromise their own hierarchy while they explain and invite people to experience in a gradual way the post-Vatican II understanding of the place of music in the liturgy.

The director of music becomes a minister of music when the person interiorizes the role of drawing forth and shaping the faith experience of the assembly in music. Nathan Mitchell sees ministers as those "who want to take the raw stuff of Christian faith and shape it into sounds that are alive, breathing, challenging and original." We associate ministry with pastoral sensitivity, which would be actualized at the 8 A.M. Mass when the professional minister has to play a piece in a key that is comfortable for morning voices rather than insisting on musical purism. One moves from director of music to minister as one begins to internalize one's relationship to the task with a call to be a servant of the Lord through whom the Lord works. In appropriating a ministerial role one does not back off from professional competency, but on the contrary one owes it to the assembly to grow professionally. The call is discerned and affirmed by the person and the assembly as each calls forth the best in the other. The very affirmation by the assembly is itself the call to ministry.

After the liturgical team has identified the musical director as a professional, a director of parish spiritual formation, liturgist, and minister, a subcommittee can begin to draw up a job description and contract. These are parish theological statements that demand the attention of the staff, parish council, and budget committee. Without a consensus from lengthy in-house dialogue we waste the time of prospective candidates and subject them to heartbreaks from misunderstandings after the person's employment begins. All must have a say in who will lead us in joyfully acclaiming the presence of the risen Christ Sunday after Sunday.

Questions for Reflection and Discussion

1. Is musical liturgy normative in our parish? Is this a goal we are moving toward?

2. What images of God are reflected in the musical texts we sing? Are they balanced, or is God continually described with only masculine characteristics? Only feminine characteristics? Only strong? Only gentle?

3. Do we have a music director? What is his or her job description? Is she or he qualified in music, liturgy, planning, communication, and spirituality? Is she or he paid a living wage? If we have only volunteer musicians, what are we saying about the importance of musical liturgy?

7

DRAMA: A LITURGICAL ART

Think of the most moving experience you have ever had at a liturgy. What was the occasion? Who was there? What did it sound, look, taste, smell, and feel like? Did it carry you into the living drama of the paschal mystery of Christ? Were your humanity and divinity touched in this experience? Were you led to further reflection on your life in Christ and on the nature of the Christian community? If you were, then in all probability this experience of liturgical prayer was rooted in sound theological, liturgical, and dramatic principles.

In order to understand the dramatic principles that go into shaping memorable experiences of liturgical prayer, consider the roots of drama, music, painting, or even liturgical prayer. These modes of expression are rooted in art. Art is humanity's interpretation of life, expressed in a way that can be universally recognized and understood. Art stirs us both emotionally and intellectually; it leaves a lasting impression that leads to further thought and reflection. A work of art does not dictate what the individual should think, but brings into consciousness the individual's own experience, images, or ideas about life.

How does this concept apply to liturgy? Liturgy can be said to be humanity's interpretation of Christian life expressed in a way that can be universally recognized and understood. Liturgy stirs us emotionally, intellectually, and spiritually. Its lasting impression leads to further thought, reflection, and prayer. Liturgy does not dictate what each person should think, but brings into consciousness one's own experiences, images, ideas and feelings about Christian life and how it can be lived out. This is further explained by Archbishop Hickey in a pastoral letter, "Let Us Give Thanks to the Lord Our God."

> The liturgy, like a good drama, seeks to involve the congregation in a deep experience of the meaning of life's joys and sorrows. The goal of liturgical experience, however, is more than the experience of personal involvement that takes place in the theatre. The liturgy grows out of and nurtures the identity of the faith community. This is why one of the goals of the liturgy is to stimulate and sustain a deep and interior religious conversion of the hearts of the participants. This conversion is the work of the Spirit of Christ. Through Him the living waters of Baptism overflow into every aspect of our personal and communal lives.[1]

Drama and dramatic production offer two different kinds of insights. The first is internal, the insight that an actor in a play achieves in order to interpret a character on stage. The second kind of insight is external, the kind a director needs in order to take the written script and transpose it into a universal experience of the essence of humanity.

Each artist has a medium of communication—painters have oils and canvas, musicians have instruments or voice—but actors have no more than body, mind, and spirit; it is through their own persons that they must communicate with others. In liturgy, the principal communicator and the principal catalyst of liturgical action is the assembly. Members of the assembly must also communicate with one another through the medium of their own bodies, minds, and spirits. Often music enhances the communication of their humanity, but there are times when communication of personal presence can only be made through the use of one's own inner resources.

Liturgical Dance and Gesture

The occasion was the wedding of a Catholic grade school instructor of dancing. If her students did not dance at the liturgical celebration of the most important event in their teacher's life, the assembly would not be giving its full expression of joy and worship. The couple sat in front of the altar after communion, while her students danced their prayer as David did before the ark.

The school janitor, affectionately known as Mush, was touched by this form of prayer and asked the students to dance at the funeral liturgy of his wife, who died painfully of cancer. This moved Mush's mother to request these children to dance at her funeral liturgy. The dance and the assembly melded. Dance that does not flow from the assembly can be disruptive entertainment, a gimmick that does not lead to prayer.

In both private and communal celebrations Catholics are increasingly experiencing the desire to engage their whole beings in prayer—body, mind, and spirit. The idea of body posture leading to an attitude, an openness to prayer, is certainly not new; religions in both the East and West have had traditions of body prayer. In our own Catholic heritage, the folding of hands, the sign of the cross, kneeling, bowing, standing, genuflecting, and prostrating have all called us to various attitudes of prayer. And as long as these body positions do not become perfunctory they can be and are very effective paths to prayer.

The liturgical committee of the Conference of Bishops in "The Arts and Body Language of Liturgy"[2] encourages and sets standards both for the gestures and bodily actions of the worshiping assembly and for the expression of bodily movement raised to the level of art through liturgical dance. The *Constitution on the Sacred Liturgy* states that to promote "active participation, the people should be encouraged to take part by means of acclamations, responses, psalms, antiphons, as well as by actions, gestures, and bodily attitudes."[3] Implementation of the first part of this directive has certainly begun. Loving, patient, and pastorally sensitive work is needed to enable congregations and their ministers to pray comfortably and unselfconsciously in bodily movement and gesture.

The Worshiper as Actor

Belief and believability are central to both the interpretive arts and the assembly of the Christian community for worship. The actor must be, first and foremost, believable in the character that he or she is portraying. The audience believes in a character more and more through believable actions, words and aspect. Something similar can be said about the members of the Christian assembly. Since the primary criterion of faith is in the question, "Do you believe?" your actions, words, and spirit must live out that belief. The words and actions of a person who does not believe or is not trying to come to belief in a liturgical assembly are just as hollow as those of an unbelievable actor. An actor calls on many inner resources to create believability. The actor must understand the character down to the spine, the motivating force. What does the character want in life? How would the character act in various circumstances? What makes the character tick? The actor enters into a truly intimate relationship with the character.

If we as members of the liturgical assembly are also serious in our beliefs, we too must spend time developing our inner resources. We must be people of prayer, both private and communal. We must want and seek a personal relationship with God and be willing to take steps to achieve this goal. We must come to know Jesus Christ, whom God has sent. How can we profess to be Christians, after all, if we

do not really know the one in whose name we act? We must be able to see everything that we do, see, think, and experience in relationship to God. What an actor brings to the performance is what we bring to liturgy.

Knowing what the character is about in the world, the actor approaches the script to determine the specific actions assigned by the playwright and to see how they fit in with the life and motivations of the character. In a similar way, the actions of the liturgical assembly have been scored for us by the church as appropriate actions for a Christian community at prayer. We gather, we speak, we listen, we respond, we bless, we break, we share, we send forth—these are our actions. As the actor interprets the character, we also have been called by the church to do these actions in the light of the people we are and hope to become. We celebrate the reality of ourselves as individuals and as a community gathered in the name of Jesus Christ. Just as different actors interpret the same role in different ways, so we too live out our call in life and at liturgy in varied and unique ways.

Once an actor has developed believability in character and understands the actions required, it is time to act. It is time to call on the power of concentration. The actor must concentrate not on self but on acting and interacting with the other actors. Foremost in mind is action, not self or emotion. We too—once we have prepared for liturgy through our inner resources of prayer and know and understand the actions of the Christian community—must finally do liturgy. We too must concentrate on the doing together. Rev. Eugene Walsh calls this "paying attention to one another." We concentrate on being present to one another in the action that is taking place here and now.

Another power that an actor must use on stage is that of observation. The actor must be aware of what is happening around him or her at all times, and must be open to reacting to it. We too, in order to gain a deeper experience of life's joys and sorrows, leading to a fuller conversion of mind and heart to Christ, need to be fully aware of what is happening around us at all times. We need to be sensitive to the sights, the sounds, the smells, the taste, and the touch of liturgy's symbols and the people all about us.

The foundation of acting is preparing and then carrying out a sequence of actions to accomplish an objective. The objective is not just getting through the play; it is much more profound. It is to reveal the significance of the characters and their actions to the meaning of life. In the same way, our belief, our actions, our "paying attention to one another," and our openness and sensitivity to what is around us are not just to get through the liturgy. These actions, this experience, should reveal the significance of our lives as individuals and as a community in Jesus Christ. As Archbishop Hickey says, "This is the work of the Spirit," but we can open or close ourselves to the movement of the Spirit. If liturgy, like drama, can make use of these internal insights, perhaps liturgy can become more often and more deeply a transforming experience for individuals and for the Christian community as a whole.

The Visual Center of Interest

After painting these large strokes with a broad brush, we begin to sort out particular aspects of the environment and art. There are many parts to the arrangement of the sacred space that create an environment and mood. One is the blocking out of the ritual action or the basic plan of movement for minister and assembly. Since all action must be both meaningful and functional, all movements must be conducive to carrying out the actions of the ritual. The functional aspect is in place if the assembly is able to see and hear, to experience the ritual. Therefore, it is the responsibility of the liturgist to highlight the important aspects of the ritual by creating a visual center of interest. This catches and holds the attention of the assembly and the other ministers so that the experience of the ritual can be felt by all.

Tools for emphasis include, first, body position. The more open a person's position, the more visual attention he or she receives. A full front is more emphatic than a quarter front; standing is more emphatic than sitting or lying; upright posture commands more attention than slouched posture.

The area assigned for action differs depending on the importance of each action to the entire ritual. Vertical level makes a difference—the higher level a minister is on, the more attention he or she receives. Levels are created by steps, the pulpit, choir bleachers, the floor, and so on.

Eye focus creates emphasis. People tend to look where others are looking. Therefore, if the presider and the cantor are both looking at the reader, so will the rest of the assembly. This is called direct focus. Indirect focus is a device for added variety—for instance, in a series in which A focuses on B who is looking at the speaking minister C.

The attention of the assembly is guided to the emphatic figure at either end of a line, depending on eye focus. The most effective visual arrangement is the triangle, whose apex is the focus of the assembly's attention. A minister surrounded by space draws more attention because of easy visibility.

A minister who is different from the others achieves dominance through contrast. On the other hand, any minister who is reinforced or backed up by minor ministers achieves emphasis. A minister can also be emphasized by the reinforcement of the environment—banners, archways, a high-backed chair, a column. A minister in a strong pool of light dominates those in dim light. The more brilliant the color of vestment or clothing, the more emphasis.

The minister in motion achieves emphasis, with the following variations. Forward movement is strong; retreating movement is weak. To accent certain words, a minister can move before uttering the line or phrase. Movement after speech stresses the action, not the words; movement during speech weakens the words and is often used when words or phrases are throwaways. The speaking minister dominates unless there is movement.

Dramatic principles can be effectively applied to any liturgy, but a good place to begin is with the peak moments and seasons of our liturgical year—the Triduum, Lent/Eastertime, Advent/Christmastime. We need to heighten awareness in the community of what liturgical prayer can be. The liturgy planning is the catalyst. Finally, we must open our eyes—some of these dramatic principles may already be in effect in our parishes. Drama is indeed a liturgical art form because it touches the heights and the depths, the emotions, the intellect, the spirit, the humanity and divinity of each one of us in Jesus Christ our Lord.

Questions for Reflection and Discussion

1. How can we as ministers develop our inner resources for the liturgy? How can we help the assembly to do the same?

2. How can we begin to use body posture and gesture at liturgy with the assembly? How will it help people to pray?

3. Why is it important for the assembly to embody its belief at the liturgy?

4. Try to analyze the focus of your liturgies. Is emphasis appropriately placed in various parts of the liturgy, or does the focus operative at your Masses work against the liturgy?

8

ENVIRONMENT AND ART

On the morning of October 4, 1979, I found myself braced against a newly planted 40-foot telephone pole, contemplating a hastily constructed platform which would serve as the space for a papal liturgy. As artistic director for the Pope's stop in Des Moines, I knew that platform inch by inch, contour upon contour. I had been haunted by its lines and textures for days. While I firmly believe the liturgy celebrated by the Pope in Des Moines was unique in conception, cooperation, interplay of elements and musicians, and visual presentation, the merits of this event must remain isolated within its own time, space, and particular geography. After all, it was a gathering for prayer of over 340,000 people (including a Pope) in a farm field somewhere in Iowa. This does not offer many opportunities for direct application. However, the hopes, ideas, and work of the many people involved constitute a valuable resource for various liturgical situations.[1]

The lesson to be learned from the Des Moines liturgy for parishes in Lookout Mountain, Tennessee, Brooklyn, New York, and Chevy Chase, Maryland is that you take the gifts of the community—their frugality or abundance —and transform them as we do the bread and wine, as the assembly is transformed into the Body of Christ. While a local community does not have the resources for a papal liturgy, the Des Moines visit of Pope John Paul remains as a watershed experience in including the best in American crafts in the liturgy.

> Care was taken not to Romanize an Iowa farm field, but rather to allow the Holy Father to be experienced as prayer leader within the context of our heritage, our best visual traditions. The lesson to be learned is that our heritage of authentic American craft elements does, indeed, have a rightful place within our liturgical experience. The craft elements in the Des Moines liturgy were many and diverse including quilting, needlework, ceramics, weaving, metal-smithing and woodworking. The items were produced by people who would not recognize themselves as "artists" but who are proud to be known as skilled crafts people. They are people able to apply imagination to their skills and push their medium to its farthest application. It is these people who, because of competence, can give credibility to the emergence of craft elements in the liturgy.[2]

The artist on the telephone pole in the Iowa cornfield is an heir to the ancient lineage of artists who embodied the faith of their communities and gave leadership to the community in every European city, town, and village in designing, building, and furnishing cathedrals, churches, and monasteries. When these buildings ceased to embody the faith of the people, they were turned into museums presided over by curators.

In this country our faith has yet to be embodied in our liturgical artifacts. We put our money into schools and churches in that order, and too often commission the architecture, building, and furnishings to people outside the community. As immigrants we were unable to translate the faith of our European and Mexican origins into an American Catholic experience. Marble statues were imported from Italy and furnishings were ordered from church goods catalogues.

Except for a rare instance like St. Patrick's in Oklahoma City where the community had a hand in the design and building, there was little community participation in making the building an expression of the living faith. For the most part our diocesan building commissions were concerned with the cost of the edifice. Liturgists were not taken seriously as consultants.

James L. Shaffer

A New Era

Vatican II was a turn-around for both music and art, evidenced in the separate documents produced by the Bishops' Committee on the Liturgy. Its 1977 document,

Environment and Art in Catholic Worship, is not a legalistic litany of "should nots," but a theological statement based on the assembly as the celebrant, which offers norms for the community as it enters a process of self-reflection about how it expresses itself in the variety of artifacts that facilitate community worship.

An important part of contemporary Church renewal is the awareness of the community's recognition of the sacred. Environment and art are to foster this awareness . . . basically, its demands are two: quality and appropriateness. Whatever the style or type, no art has a right to a place in liturgical celebration if it is not of high quality and if it is not appropriate.

Quality is perceived only by contemplation, by standing back from things and really trying to see them, trying to let them speak to the beholder. Cultural habit has conditioned the contemporary person to look at things in a more pragmatic way: "What is it worth?" "What will it do?" Contemplation sees the hand stamp of the artist, the honesty and care that went into an object's making, the pleasing form and color and texture. Quality means love and care in the making of something, honesty and genuineness with any materials used, and the artist's special gift in producing a harmonious whole, a well-crafted work. This applies to music, architecture, sculpture, painting, pottery making, furniture making, as well as to dance, mime or drama—in other words, to any art form that might be employed in the liturgical environment or action.

Appropriateness is another demand that liturgy rightfully makes upon any art that would serve its action. The work of art must be appropriate in two ways: 1) it must be capable of bearing the weight of mystery, awe, reverence, and wonder which the liturgical action expresses; 2) it must clearly serve (and not interrupt) ritual actions which have their own structure, rhythm and movement.

The first point rules out anything trivial and self-centered, anything fake, cheap or shoddy, anything pretentious or superficial. That kind of appropriateness, obviously, is related to quality. But it demands more than quality. It demands a kind of transparency, so that we see and experience both the work of art and something beyond it.

By environment we mean the larger space in which the action of the assembly takes place. At its broadest, it is the setting of the building in its neighborhood, including outdoor spaces. More specifically it means the character of a particular space and how it affects the action of the assembly. There are elements in the environment, therefore, which contribute to the overall experience, e.g., the seating arrangement, the placement of liturgical centers of action, temporary decoration, light, acoustics, spaciousness, etc. The environment is appropriate when it is beautiful, when it is hospitable, when it clearly invites and needs an assembly of people to complete it.[3]

The Artist as Consultant

As Prior of an Augustinian house of formation, I asked an artist, Lillian Brulc, to consider the redesign of our chapel. When she met with the community, she offered no suggestions. She simply acted as a facilitator. "What do you want to do? Why?" She was drawing out of us our theology of worship. She did this most effectively when she asked about specifics: lighting, floor covering, chairs, and altar. The choice of each option was a statement about how we imaged God, worship, and prayer. She made it clear that she was not offering suggestions. It would be presumptous for her to tell us what suited our prayer life when she had not experienced it through day-to-day living.

Her experience, not only as an artist and Old Testament scholar but also as a worker in both Latin America and urban North America, was the background for her discipline in not projecting on the community what she thought would be best for us. It forced the community to see the chasm in their differences in theology and worship and postpone any remodeling of the chapel until they bridged their differences in their understanding of prayer.

A major role of the liturgical artist as consultant to the assembly is to draw out and lift up what the community is saying about itself. The architect can then translate into drawings what she or he discerns as the heart beat of the assembly so that the community can see if it properly mirrors itself in the drawings. It is arrogance for an artist to tell an assembly what is best for them or to permit them to abdicate their responsibility.

A few years later at St. Victor's I invited Father Robert Hovda, a liturgist with a keen eye for environment and art, to visit the church. His response was simply a socratic question, "How is it we pay attention to the front of the church and do nothing about the rest?" Why do we arrange our banners and flowers around the altar and not concern ourselves with the body of the church? The key to the answer is where we place the focus of the celebration. If it is the priest offering Mass for the congregation, the focus is the altar. If it is the assembly that celebrates the presence of the risen Lord, the focus is switched to where the assembly is located. With this shift in theology, there would be a switch in the focus of the lighting. We might rethink our use of banners and consider using them, as does Rockefeller Chapel in Chicago, as pendants hanging throughout the church drawing the attention to the people.

In the zeal of beginners to brighten or liven up the space there is the temptation to use banners indiscriminately, as though they were entities in themselves. A banner should be used for more than reflecting itself. Rather, it should feed into the season and be used as a reinforcement of a particular role. A typical altar might have a crucifix and two banners on either side with no one in front of them to be reinforced. The height of the banner in back of the lector or in front of the lectern can reinforce the person proclaiming the word. Musicians more often than lectors lack the reinforcement that is concentrated on the altar and the presider.

The assembly can be called upon to contribute to creating an environment that speaks to the community. In any large group there are people with a wide assortment of artistic talents, especially those who have no awareness of their giftedness until they are encouraged to pledge themselves to work for an environment that will reveal the sacred to the worshipers. To bring God from a distant supreme being to one whose warmth and penetrating presence is felt through the skill of local artists is a kind of miracle an art and environment committee can perform. The St. Victor banner committee is a group of people with a variety of skills who are willing to meet week after week and prepare the community for worship through the rich variety of the liturgical seasons and special occasions.

The banner committee answers for the parish the questions the Jewish people ask at the Seder meals, "Why is this meal different from every other meal?" Banners for every season can set the mood for the congregation before the commentator or leader of song comes to the podium. Like the hieroglyphics on the wall of the ancient catacombs, banners serve as teachers for people who have only one hour a week with the church.

The Gifted Among Us

In the banner committee the people who feel ungifted as artists cut, sew, measure, hang, and soon become aware that these humble tasks share in the giftedness of the group. Ideally the group needs someone with a historical sense of the liturgy and a scripture background, but we live in a real world and settle for people who will do minimal reading that will inform them of the thrust of the season or the feast.

Without the input of a trained person or the lack of a study club approach to the work, the liturgical planning team will be muted in this area. The banners will have a tendency to be wordy or sentimental and will not bring us to prayer through our rich liturgical heritage. If there is no one in the group with a sense of liturgical history and scripture, the liturgist, a qualified staff member, or a

member of the planning team would be a necessary resource or liaison. Practical details like work space, storage
space, and materials must be brokered with the financial
committee. The resolution, like all budget items, will be a
value issue.

Senior groups can be brought into the work of creating
an environment for worship through special projects. At St.
Thomas Apostle Parish in Chicago, a group of seniors spent
the entire season of Lent preparing a quilted banner for
Holy Week. Each senior was to express in his or her block of
quilt an understanding of the theme of Lent of the particular year. Seniors who spent a large part of the year preparing for the arts and craft senior bazaar can be drawn into
the building of the house of worship. The person skilled in
stitchery can ornament the lectionary. When one's imagination is freed to feel there is a place for each one's contribution to the environment, the possibilities are endless.

Questions for Reflection and Discussion

1. Do we respect and call forth the gifts of craftspeople and
artists in our parish?

2. Are we conscious of our worship environment? What does our
church building say about our theology of church? Have we
considered our seating arrangement? What about the centers of
liturgical action? If the assembly is the primary symbol of Christ at
the Mass, does our art and environment point to that fact, or do
we just decorate the sanctuary?

3. The quality of art is not measured in dollars and cents, but by
honesty and giftedness. Have we evaluated our liturgical art
pieces in this light?

4. All works of liturgical art must be appropriate, not just functional, to the liturgical action. Have we evaluated the appropriateness of our art?

5. Do we have a parish art and environment committee or coordinator? Why is such a ministry needed in our parish? How is this different from a banner committee?

9

THE GATHERING

If we accept the eucharist as a table ritual, then we are assuming that people are not simply coming to hear a lecture, to be moved by the aesthetics of tasteful art, to be moved by good music, or to enter into contemplative prayer. All of the above are important to focus and heighten the purpose for which we are gathered, that is, the sharing of a meal to become a community in the name of the Lord Jesus.

The gathering begins as people leave their cars and walk toward the church. I have a fantasy of what might happen if we had mimes or clowns who would be in the parking lot fifteen minutes before every weekend liturgy. The sole purpose would be to make people laugh by making them aware of their seriousness, to help them to meet the Lord of the Dance, who might loosen up their bodies, and to let the Lord of History take responsibility for his world for the next hour. High school students could make a project of opening doors for people. Parents of small children could turn their kids loose on the people as they walked toward the church to elicit joy and laughter.

We have a long tradition of church as serious business: a time to pay a debt or an opportunity to enter the holy of holies as individuals rather than a body of people. We have conflicting traditions. One tradition sees the assembly of people as a public celebration. The secular model would be a political rally where people come to receive the energies needed to carry out the campaign. Another would be a liturgy in the plaza of a Catholic town or village where everyone is gathered after an afternoon of conversation, games, eating, and drinking. The image closer to the early church is that of believers meeting in the upper room of a home. There would be conversation or small talk we all engage in when we meet friends. We talk about the health of ourselves and members of our immediate family, our work, our play, our neighbors. It is through these simple exchanges that we build the kind of relationship needed to be at ease with one another.

There is another tradition that sees the church not as a house but as the holy of holies. There is an unresolved tension between seeing the church as a place of devotion and as a house of public worship. My early recollection of church, which comes from my mother and my first grade teacher, each reinforcing the other, was that Jesus lived in the tabernacle and it was a sin to talk in church. The eucharistic piety of older people centered on the tabernacle, focused on the tabernacle lamp. Devotion to the blessed sacrament with benediction after Mass and the Forty Hours Devotion focused on the tabernacle rather than the altar. The church of Vatican II has not succeeded in resolving the tension of preserving a tradition of Catholic piety which has power to continue to nourish burnt-out activists and people who want to deepen their prayer life, and at the same time having the church become a family gathered around a table for a festive meal and celebration. We must still search to find creative ways of preserving both values.

As people come to Mass on Sunday they take holy water at the door, genuflect, kneel for a few moments of prayer, and then sit reflectively waiting for the gathering rite to begin. As a parish priest I am caught between two traditions. I want to welcome people in the church in the fifteen minutes before the service, and at the same time I want to honor those who do not want to be distracted by my welcoming. I have worked out a pastoral compromise. While not usurping the role of usher I move slowly up and down the aisles paying attention to the children, asking them their names and engaging in playful interchanges in a way that does not disturb people bowed in meditation. As I move through the aisles I give nods of recognition to people who wish to engage me in eye contact and exchange smiles. A parishioner told me that this was more important than my homilies, reinforcing the importance of gestures or symbolic action over words. Attitudes are mediated by what we do rather than by what we say.

Ushers: The Official Greeters

It is the ministry of ushers to be the official greeters of the assembly. Ideally, ushers are outgoing people who have a sensitivity to people and who exude a warmth that signals a gracious welcome. They are people who are called upon to assume responsibility for a variety of needs: windows to be closed or opened, bulletins to be distributed, people to be helped to seats. Ushers gently but forcefully are assertive in using their crowd control skills. The collection is to be taken up. Gift bearers are to be appointed and in place. Lost and found articles are reported to them. The list of chores may seem overwhelming, but for an experienced usher they fall in place with the ease of a seasoned ballplayer moving under a long fly near the centerfield fence. The overarching focus of the varied chores of the usher is to help the people come together as a prayerful, loving community.

The ministry of ushers is different from ushering in a theater, but not because one is sacred and the other secular. The theater usher is helping people as individuals to achieve individual goals as well as protecting individuals from the tyranny of a crowd. The usher as a liturgical minister uses many of the skills of a theater usher, but his goal is to help knit individual worshipers into a community that will pray together. If he is a caring person, he will be able to listen to the concerns and complaints of the people and act as a liaison, feeding back to the staff information that might be helpful to them as liturgy ministers and pastors. They can inform the janitorial staff of the small items that need repair or attention and pass on information about jobs wanted and job openings.

Ushers have been taken for granted, as housewives were before the feminist movement. The institution of ushering is as old as the parish church: ushers were there opening doors on the day of the first Mass in its first public building. The training of ushers took place without a work-shop on the role of ushers. It was handed down by older men showing the younger men where to find things and what to do with them. An usher was like a priest before the era of liturgical renewal who took his directions solely from the red print in the missal without any reference to how he

Lou Niznik

was received by an assembly of people from which his prayer service should elicit a response.

In the post-Vatican era there were sabbaticals, seminars, and workshops for the retraining of priests. With the post-Vatican II ministries of lector, musician, and minister of communion, the task was training rather than retraining. New wine did not have to be poured into old wine skins. The men of good will who opened and closed the church and did the difficult backstage chores were left in the vestibule while other ministers studiously applied Vatican II theology to liturgical practice in the parish. There is no association of ushers that conducts retraining institutes for them. They stand inside church doors awaiting the ministry of the staff to initiate training sessions to bring them into full liturgical participation with the assembly so that they might be singing as they are helping form the communion lines or as they escort the gift bearers to the altar. If they worked in tandem with the musicians they could help people find the right page in the right song book as the ushers themselves modeled participation. The parish liturgist or the parish liturgical team needs to sit down with the ushers to design a retraining program. The generous people who were the insiders before Vatican II and later became outsiders must be restored to their place as insiders in the renewed church.

Sexism was not an issue when churches were founded earlier in this century. Just as women's place was in the kitchen, the usher's room was for men only. There is no Vatican decree that says that women cannot be ushers. In an era where women drive buses, wear police uniforms, are waitresses and hostesses in restaurants and ushers in theaters, there is no liturgical or cultural reasons why women should not share this role with men. The airlines show us that men and women can serve in the same crew in ushering people to their seats and doing other functions common to ushers. Each diocese and parish needs to design, implement, and oversee its own affirmative action program. Social change or liturgical change does not just happen. The pastoral team might hesitate because of possible negative reactions. This indeed may be an ungrounded fear. The parishioners of St. Victor's enthusiastically accepted female ushers with the feeling that at last the church was becoming human.

The Gathering Rite

The procession is designed to be the focus of the ritual gathering. It calls people to leave their private prayers or their chatting and come together as an assembly to hear the story and break the bread. The size of the space and the number of people in the assembly will have a bearing on the number of people and roles represented in the procession. A full complement would include cross bearer, acolytes, book bearer, and ministers of the eucharist.

If the entrance rite or procession is done with dignity, the people pick up the feeling that something important is to begin as the procession moves with an unhurried gait, neither casual nor pompous. The assembly has the feeling of being led into sacred precincts. If the liturgy is less formational, the presider or the one who prepares people for the gathering needs to work at creating the sense of awe necessary to approach the mystery. The focus of the procession is not the presider, who may feel called to attract attention to himself by his styled vestments or a casual or pompous posture. He simply reflects all the celebrants, which is the assembly. His vestments are designed to emphasize his role rather than attract attention to himself. While the manner of wearing the vestments reflects the personality of the celebrant, the overarching concern is that the vestments link the assembly to a twenty-century tradition. The purpose of the gathering rite is to gather the people together as a community of believers and prepare them for the hearing of the word.

If a reader has to follow a greeting, penitential rite, Gloria, and opening prayer, all flatly read without music or silence intervening, he or she is more apt than not to face a congregation already saturated with words, unprepared to receive the word he or she has to proclaim.

On the other hand, a bracing entrance song, with a real procession of ministers through the church, a warm greeting, a muted penitential rite, a triumphant Gloria sung with enthusiasm, an opening prayer said with deliberate pacing (preceded by and followed with a generous silent pause) can all aid in putting a congregation into a prayerful and receptive mood. People need a warming-up period before a liturgy can get under way, and such preliminary prayers and gestures are indispensable for this.

Here, the presider has a particular responsibility to prepare the way for the reader. If his or her gestures are cramped and furtive or over-hasty (the rush from sacristy to altar instead of a real procession, the quick greeting, the careless opening prayer), he or she is suggesting that we are starting something we had best be done with as soon as possible. On the other hand, if the presider honors the congregation with a solemn entry, a friendly greeting, and a measured prayer, he or she is telling everyone that we are getting ready for something important. Then, when the presider sits to hear the readings, everyone else will sit back mentally as well as physically, and be ready to listen with him or her.

The musicians should also be alert not to weary the assembly with an excessively lengthy entrance song, nor to distract them with one which is inappropriate to an entrance procession. It should be brisk, lively, and not oversolemn, even in penitential seasons. Nor should congregations be wearied with the all-too-frequent recitation of the Gloria. This is an acclamatory hymn or anthem, and all the Kyrie before it is a song of welcome and acknowledgment of the risen Lord present in the gathered assembly.[1]

Questions for Reflection and Discussion

1. Have we re-evaluated the role of usher in our parish since the

Vatican II implementations? Have ushers ever been trained in their new ministry?

2. How do we become a gathered community each week? What actions do we do together to become gathered at Mass?

3. Many liturgical ministers are involved in the Rite of Gathering. What is the specific function of each one during this time? Are they aware that their ministry at this time is gathering?

10

THE PRESIDER

When did the church switch the title of the priest offering a Mass from celebrant to presider? The question box answer is 1973, when the church issued the new missal with detailed instructions that grounded its changes in a Vatican II theology.

> The celebration of the eucharist is the action of the whole church, in which each individual should take his own full part and only his part as determined by his particular position in the people of God. In this way greater attention is given to some aspects of the eucharistic celebration which have sometimes been overlooked in the course of time. The worshipping community is the people of God, won by Christ with his blood, called together by the Lord, and nourished by his word.[1]

The emphasis in this statement is on the assembly itself, of which the priest is a member, that celebrates. He presides in, not over, the celebration.

Prior to the *General Instruction of the Roman Missal* it was the priest who celebrated for the people. He was the Moses who hid his face from the people because of the dazzling light of being in God's holy presence. With his back turned to them during the eucharistic prayer he refracted that light into their lives. He was the mediator between God and humankind. In the language of the nineteenth-century French preacher Bousset, he brought God to people and people to God. The radical switch of the Council emphasized the Lord revealing himself in the paschal mystery through the faith of the assembly of which the priest is a part and in which he presides.

His hands were facing each other at shoulder width. From the consecration to finishing the distribution of communion his thumb and index finger were joined because they had touched the sacred species and could not be used to turn the pages until they were purified. When he turned to greet the people with a *Dominus vobiscum* he dug his elbows into his sides and opened them to shoulder width with palms facing each other and his eyes on the floor lest he lose his footing or see the people in front of him. Expansive gestures and eye contact would reveal his humanity and detract from the people's experiencing the holy in its purest form, unpolluted by the pecularities of a human who otherwise represented Christ.

In shifting from celebrant to presider we are shifting theological perspectives of glacial proportions. We will not survive unless our seat buckles are securely fastened. The shift reveals a change in how the church sees God's presence revealed in human life. The old theology did not allow the priest to interfere with each person's communion with the Lord. The quiet Mass with the celebrant keeping his personhood in wraps was able to mediate the divine without human interference. It reflects an authentic strain in the history of Catholic spirituality. While the liturgy must indeed lead us to the transcendent, today we believe that in a liturgical setting it can be best mediated through a community, including the presider, that expresses its humanity in the service itself.

The liturgy as a celebration of life may be best illus-

Lou Niznik

trated in a funeral liturgy, particularly of an elderly person
whose life was perceived as precious to the community. The
mourners want to find the presence of Christ in their remembrance. The liturgy can be used to enshrine these
memories in a living, vital, holy remembrance of the deceased, warts and all. The celebration of the liturgy begins
at the wake. As we mingle with the mourners, we share our
faith with one another as we recall the words and deeds of
the deceased and express our feelings to the family. If we
stay long enough and meet friends of the deceased, we
share stories, the anecdotes that bring out the foibles and
idiosyncrasies as well as the greatness of the deceased. Our
acceptance or love is not total until we can face up to and
etch the flaws into the mosaic.

The community will meet again for the liturgy. The
presider will lift up, not his feelings alone, but the feelings
and faith the people share with one another at the wake. It
truly becomes a celebration when the presider allows the
faith of the people to speak in the moments of silence, in his

reverent but relaxed gestures, the way he enunciates the name of the deceased in the opening prayer. He is walking, sitting, standing, and praying with the assembly. Unlike the soloist in an orchestra, he does not attract attention to himself, but is reflecting or deflecting what is happening in the assembly. The difference between the studied self-demeaning posture of the celebrant of a previous era and the expansive human touch of the present is designedly invitational.

The Symphony Conductor

The presider is inviting the community through his warmth, openness, and gentle use of the authority invested in him by the assembly and total church to join in letting their feelings flow like a river. He is a conductor who as humanly but as unobtrusively as possible blends the faith and feelings of the community into the worship of the Father who gifted the deceased with life before and after death. When the presider uses his role to flaunt his humanity or tease responses from the worshippers, he betrays his understanding of how a presider uses his humanity. It should not be used to separate him from the community, but for the community to become aware of its own humanity and be at one with the collective humanity of the assembly.

In the seminary of my era the test of being a good presider was adherence to a manual. It was a translation from a German author who could have written the manuals for training in the Prussian army. When hands were joined, the right thumb was to be over the left, a simple clue to how the presider was to see himself when he put on his uniform. It never occurred to the trainers to have an audience for the dry run before ordination. It was like taking a driver's test without getting into the driver's seat and experiencing the open road. Now the presider is asked to be the leader of a prayer community and must experience himself as one relating to people every moment, rather than keeping his head in the book to read the directions properly.

Today the primary requirement of the leader is that the person be a fully developed human being with a capacity to respond to the life around him and channel that life through the ritual action around which the people have gathered. It is the articulation of the spirituality of St. Cyprian's crisp sentence: "The glory of God is the Christian fully alive." The presider has switched from the clerical robot to the fully developed human sensitive to life around him. The presider must be sensitive to the feelings he is experiencing at the moment and with this self-awareness he must be capable of experiencing the feelings of the people in front of him as he stands in the pulpit and around him when at the altar. A finely tuned leader is one who is constantly reading the thermometer of feelings as the mercury rises and falls with the mood changes in himself and the assembly. There is no crash course that can make one a growing person with this heightened sense of awareness of feelings and the ability to respond spontaneously at every moment. This is not a prerogative of age or sex; it is a charism. Some ungifted people with training can preside in such a way that the Lord can work through them in spite of their limitations. Others are so ungifted that training is a source of frustration for the trainer, the trainee, but most important for the assembly. The untrainable, ungifted has the power to destroy a praying community.

A presider may have internalized a childhood role of presider as one with a pious mien with head slightly tilted to the left and shoulders rounded and slightly stooped or bowed. One such prelate with hands folded, head tilted slightly forward and to the left managed to keep his posture as he stood beside the pope, who was waving and smiling radiantly as he responded to the cheers of hundreds of thousands of people. The prelate's posture became known as "ten to twelve." Although a warm and compassionate person, his understanding of presider did not allow him to incorporate his humanity into the liturgy. For some priests, otherwise alive and loving, the natural expression of their humanity is perceived as a betrayal of their priesthood.

An Integrated Humanity

To let one's humanity show through is not an easy exercise for one in middle life. When I became a clinical pastoral education intern at a university hospital, I decided that I would try out my humanity by wearing a shirt and tie rather than the traditional clerical uniform that I had worn for thirty years. It was not a case of hiding my identity as a chaplain; I wore "Chaplain Geaney" as a badge on the lapel of my hospital coat. As the weeks passed and my supervisor studied my verbatim pastoral reports, he concluded that I was still "Father" Geaney in the hospital room, which interpreted meant that I was into the "six minutes of twelve" role with the pious mien, submissive posture of the stereotypical preacher. The supervisor said, "When you are with your peers in the staff room you are a lot of fun, but when you are on the floor you become a piece of church furniture." It was a heavy judgment. The tie did not make me automatically human; it was neither an obstacle nor a help. It did not get me out of the heavily laden clerical posture that interferes with offering the sacramental presence of the human person I am.

The growing awareness that the greatest gift I could give to a patient was sharing my broken humanity, was a painfully slow process. I could better minister through the tears and laughter of an open personhood than the layers of protectiveness that the clerical role had built into my ministering style. I learned that patients were not aware of my identity crisis and cared not whether I was wearing a tie or a clerical collar if I could hold their hand and be present to them as a fellow pilgrim sharing my humanity as we walked through the valley of darkness. Easier said or written than done! As Keifer writes:

> We are all subliminally aware that the present liturgy lacks power. It is all too rarely a source of real nourishment for people's life in the world, as it is rarely experienced as fully celebrating that life. Only the brighter and tamer emotions are admitted. My colleagues often locate this liturgical blandness in a

bland use of symbol—the failure to use real bread, robust gesture, generous art. But the failure of ceremonial symbols is rooted in a deeper failure of symbol. The primary liturgical symbols are not the liturgical artifacts and gestures, but its *agents,* especially its ministers and above all its priests . . . . To the extent that the priest embodies (if only potentially) the values, hopes, and aspirations of a community, to that extent is he a "good celebrant," and to that extent is there the possibility òf a liturgy with dynamic power.[2]

Since the present discipline of the church allows only males to preside in the liturgy, it becomes crucially important that there are women in the procession and at the altar in a variety of roles to compensate for the males' inability to symbolize and embody the feelings, hopes, and aspirations of women. After a Sunday liturgy in which I presided as a visitor, a middle-aged woman came to the pastor and spoke with deep emotion: "This was one of the most moving experiences I have ever had in church and will always remember. When I saw two girls in the sanctuary I wept. When I was their age I wept in bed because I could not do what they were doing today."

The liturgical procession should be as representative as a New York City Democratic party slate of candidates, which is representative of each major ethnic, racial, and religious voting block. While this variety of ministers is desirable, it cannot distract us from the focus of attention of the faith and humanity of the presider. A deep faith and an expansive humanity do not come from a liturgical practicum but from life experience. It is the accumulation of spirit moments as we make choices each day. Our faith and humanity at any moment of our history are the summation or incarnation of how we faced, acted out, and interpreted the events of life.

Wisdom People

What matters is not the initial assessment of the success or failure of an event, but how we integrate it into the totality

of our lives. Life experiences close as well as open us to
life. While age does not guarantee wisdom, the apostle Paul
had a bias toward older and married men as presiders in the
community (I Timothy 3: 1-3).

While the selection of ministers for the assembly will
focus on readiness for ministry based on the maturity Paul
alludes to in the letter to Timothy, one can acquire great
proficiency in relational skills through a variety of leadership and listening workshops and seminars. However, if a
person does not have some charisma for relating, it can be a
frustrating experience for all.

An effective presider is a listener. Although listening is
a basic ministerial skill, the presider of a particular assembly
would do well to arrive on the scene when the first wave of
people are moving toward the church, probably fifteen
minutes before the liturgy. This time can be spent in the
parking lot greeting the early arrivers, going up and down
the aisles, or standing at the church entrance before vest-
ing. He is welcoming, creating a joyful mood, but he is also
listening in a way that helps him to vibrate with their
thoughts and feelings.

The Presider in Procession

As he walks in procession the finely tuned presider has the
feeling that he is one with the people. It is reflected in his
body movements as he walks, songbook in hand, singing. If
he is happy to be with them in this role, his face is beaming
and his feelings are reflected in the smile that goes from
one person to another as he passes each bench. When he
arrives at the altar, continues singing, and then greets the
people, the smiles and good feelings of being together feed
back to him in their response. If the response is simply a
grunt or a mechanical ritual response, it means that he has
not picked up the joy of the people and relayed it back to
them. He is neither feeding nor being fed, which argues
that it will be a peanut butter and jelly sandwich rather than
a delightfully prepared and relaxed dinner. It may be that
he has not given them permission to respond warmly to his
warm greeting.

In the warming-up process before the procession begins, in the procession itself, and in the opening greeting, the presider's eyes are not on the stained glass windows or the joining of the beams of the roof of the church but on the people around him and in front of him. It is registering with him in an unreflected way that the people at this particular Mass are elderly, middle-aged and married, young and single, or whatever the particular blend at this Mass. This will have a subtle effect on his tone of voice and how he tells a particular story. He must not only relate warmly to the assembly, but needs to know the mindsets and thought patterns of the people.

Jimmy Walker, the legendary and charming Mayor of New York City in the early part of this century, found himself at a podium speaking to a group whose identity he forgot to inquire about. If he only knew to whom he was speaking, he could tailor the message. He began by touching in casual fashion New York symbols. As soon as the audience would respond enthusiastically to a particular symbol it would identify them and he could address himself to their concerns.

The verbal images and speech patterns we use are as symbolic as the clothes we wear. Like Jimmy Walker, the skilled presider adapts himself to his audience. While the liturgy committee may have written the score weeks ahead, and the preachers prayed over and read the scriptures in preparing their homilies, we begin to switch, add, eliminate examples, or more likely, to nuance them differently as we move through the liturgy. In this sense every liturgy is dialogical. If we are particularly sensitive to the mood of the assembly and pick up its rhythm, energy is generated and moves in different directions as particular emotions are evoked.

The presider may not be one with the people in his celibate and rectory lifestyle, but from living among them he knows the words that turn them off and on, the images that they are familiar with, the kinds of stories or allusions that they like to hear or not hear.

The procession is about to begin. I notice a couple coming in. The husband is taking a course in miracles that has a different theological base than mine. The word has a very different meaning for him than for me. In fact, "miracle" is charged with many meanings. I was going to use the miraculous in a negative sense in one of my examples. If I said, as I had planned to, that "God works through the human rather than the miraculous," I would needlessly turn him off and probably many others. I switched to "God does not wave a magic wand over us." My homily was not watered down, but refined by his presence. It expressed my thought more precisely.

At another liturgy I am walking in the procession and I say to myself, "I did not realize so many elderly people go to this Mass." It is not a question of rewriting the homily or even more consciously reflecting on this datum. It will be played out while I am in the pulpit. I continue up the aisle, looking at and greeting the people as I pass. I listen to the first reading and prayerfully let myself be present to myself and the Lord in the cantor's responsory. I am in a state of absorption. I am receiving, not thinking or planning changes in the homily; but the homily is changing. The way I speak each word, each sentence, is a response to how I am receiving these people and how they are receiving me. Whether I am flat or alive depends as much on them as me. Dancers take time to find the rhythm to which they can move together. Every performance is not brilliant, but I have an awareness of what might be happening to us even as the alleluia verse is being sung. I stand at the pulpit poised to proclaim the word, the possibility of igniting myself with the congregation enhanced. Afterward I wonder why I said this or that, left something out or added something else. I was allowing room for the Spirit as I glided through the homily with the people in my embrace.

It is the homily itself that has the greatest possibility of establishing rapport and oneness between people and presider and among the people themselves. The homily has the potential to evoke common images that identify the nitty gritty of family, work, or community living that relates them to the sacred. At the eucharistic prayer in a Sunday liturgy I saw a man in the middle of the church leaning forward with intensity, as though poised as a sprinter to leap forward to be present with me at the altar. Before he received the eucharist in his hand he said, "Thank you for the homily." It was clear now that it was the homily that pulled him into the eucharistic prayer. Somehow the prayer of the assembly was ritualizing and carrying forward the word that was spoken to him from the pulpit.

Since the presider or homilist is a highly symbolic person, it is often the images he evokes rather than the logic of his message that is the carrier of the word. An inarticulate homilist at times communicates the word through warmth and gestures, with loving feelings compensating for a clear and developed presentation. In the absence of sensitive presiders, music and ritual may be seen as a fall-back, saving the service from complete disaster.

We are not trying to establish an order of effectiveness between the celebrative presence of the presider, the effectiveness of the homilist, the penetration of the music, the awfulness of silence, and the power of ritual itself. Each is a part of a larger symphony, the strength of one supplying at times for the weakness of another. It is psychologically damaging for the assembly to demand perfection of itself in each area.

Questions for Reflection and Discussion

1. What qualities make a presider effective in his role at Mass?

2. Have our various presiders ever been helped in their liturgical ministry since the Vatican II implementations? Have they ever been videotaped or tape-recorded and been helped to become aware of their assets and liabilities as presiders?

3. Should a presider change his style of presiding at various Masses? Why? In what types of groups would a different style be helpful? How would his style change with each of these assemblies?

11

THE SERVICE OF THE WORD

When the reader walks to the podium, she is presenting herself to an assembly that may or may not be prepared for the readings. The people are waiting for someone to proclaim to them the word in accents that will reverberate in the marrow of their bones and set them on fire with a vision of what life could be like. Or it may be that the assembly has been so domesticated by dull renditions of the good news that their expectations are simply to hear the words, however poorly enunciated and strung together. In previous chapters we raised a number of questions. Is the assembly prepared through its ministry of hospitality and its gathering ritual to hear the word? In this chapter we ask what is required for effective reading and how readers are chosen. Is the reader who has accepted this ministry one who inwardly identifies as a minister of the word and has remotely and proximately prepared to be the channel of the word?

The Reader

The train conductor who calls the stops in a staccato tone may have an excellent voice and do his job well, but he makes a poor reader at a liturgical service. The bible is not read like a list of stops on Amtrak, a recipe book, or a telephone directory. The bible is a book that contains the stories of God that the reader must make come alive as the entire liturgy makes present Jesus Christ among us. The Liturgy of the Word is a part of an orchestrated drama that brings people to the depths of themselves where they touch the Lord in the midst of the assembly. The reader must be able to enunciate the words so that each syllable has time to resound in every part of the church, and at the same time, to grasp with his or her eye the arrangement of the phrases, sentences, and paragraphs. The reader must give importance to verbs and nouns over adverbs and adjectives and downplay articles and prepositions.

> Readers should be persons who can conduct themselves with decorum before an assembly, who can walk without shuffling and stand without slouching, who can, in short, act with poise before a gathering of people. If the reader is obviously uncomfortable before an assembly of people, or cannot read in such a way as to be heard easily, the assembly will experience his or her sense of failure, and not the proclamation of the Word. The reader should also be a person who projects a sense of warmth and empathy with the assembly without seeming overbearing, folksy and preachy.[1]

The most obvious skill we have pointed to in our description of the role of reader is proficiency in public reading at the elementary level of pronouncing the words audibly. A second level is the incorporation in the reader of the insights from the dramatic arts as they apply to the liturgy. Several internal techniques of drama can be used effectively by specialized ministers to help create for all a moving experience of prayer. These techniques are especially useful to cantors and lectors, but other ministers may also profit from using them.

Sense Recall

The first internal technique is called "sense recall." It involves three steps: having a sensory experience, remembering the sensory experience, and transferring the essence of the experience to the present moment. The goal is to make more real, or more alive, a sensory image that is being

Lou Niznik

spoken or sung about. Suppose you are asked to proclaim the Ezekiel "dry bones" reading. Concentrating on the sensory imagery of dryness, you may try to recall an experience of brittleness or dryness—piles of dry autumn leaves all over the lawn, for example, or the arid land of the Arizona or California deserts. Once you have named the experience, remember it clearly in your mind and feel it in your body. What did it look, smell, feel like? What was your reaction to it? When you have been able to recapture for yourself the essence of the vision, transfer this sensory impression and feeling to your reading about the dry bones. When you proclaim the passage, see the dry bones as you saw the leaves or the desert. Let your senses respond again the way they did in the original experience. This will in turn help your listeners to experience the same dryness, adding to the intensity and the impact of the reading on their lives.

Emotional Recall

The second internal technique, emotional recall, is related to the first. This technique involves the same three steps of having the experience, recalling the experience, and transferring the essence of the experience to the present moment. For example, a cantor is asked to pray Psalm 22 at a liturgy: "God my God, why have you deserted me? . . . I call all day, my God, but you never answer. . . ." The cantor who is not currently experiencing the depth of these emotions seeks a way to interpret and pray the psalm meaningfully and truthfully for and with the gathered assembly. The key again is to return to personal experiences for a time and place and situation in which the same kind of deep emotions were experienced. The key to emotional recall is to remember the whole experience, not just the emotion associated with it. You must remember where it took place, with whom, why, what the day was like, and so on. As you remember the associations of the experience in more and more detail, the emotion will come to the singing of the psalm. Again, when singing, do not remember the feeling, but see and remember the context of the experience itself; from this recollection, the feeling will come.

Neither of these techniques involves any kind of pretending; on the contrary, both use genuine life experiences to interpret the universal human experience. Rather than being fake or phony, these methods contribute to making the experience of liturgical prayer genuinely human and real.

Beyond the simple enunciation of the words and the use of the dramatic arts, the ministry of reader could lead to the assimilation of the word so that the reader is not an actor with a script in hand, but a believer in word and deed of what she proclaims. When a person says a reader is too dramatic, this is often meant in a pejorative sense, meaning that the person was not true to herself, adopting a false style or imitating someone else. The goal is for the reader to bring together what she proclaims and what is human in the reader in an interplay that helps people to pray. The reader offers a genuine humanity as a filter through which the hearer can experience the message in another person.

An understanding of the scriptures is required so that when one reads the hearer feels that the message has been understood and interiorized by the reader. Ideally the reader is making a belief statement. In order to achieve this ideal, the reader should spend some time in the study and reading of scriptures. There is a rapidly expanding library of tapes and short books explaining particular books of the bible. For example, an introduction to the writings of Paul would help a reader get a feel for his didactic style, which differs from the styles of gospel stories and prophetic utterances.

Who Should Be Chosen?

The people who are chosen to proclaim the word of God must exemplify this word in the community. What they read must have filtered into their lives in such a way that people sense that the person at the lectern not only reads well but really believes what she is proclaiming. No one can define the behavior of such a Christian, but everyone can recognize its presence or absence. It is evident in her bearing. We select people with possibilities for development who are willing to submit to a training course and willing to be criticized and able to take a hint that they might better serve in another ministry.

How Are Readers Chosen?

While the office of lector officially recognized by the church is reserved for men, the simple designation as reader is adequate for a church that at grassroots is decreasingly concerned with status, sex, and title.

The reader is the community proclaiming its message to itself. Since the reader is speaking for the community, he or she should not only be a member of the community, but a representative of one of the many segments of its composition. No one person in the lector's stand can symbolize a man and woman; young, middle-aged and old; White, Brown, and Black. Yet we do need role models in the lector's stand. It is a powerful reason why priests, sisters, professional ministers, and professional newscasters should do the reading sparingly. The team of readers should be representative of the sexes, ages, nationalities, and races of the parishioners, but as we pointed out in an earlier chapter, representative of particular assemblies.

The elderly person is speaking to the elderly as a peer and to the young as the wise people they can grow into. The young person is telling youth that they belong and reassuring the elders that their precious heritage will be preserved. The Black or Hispanic in a predominantly White congregation is affirming his or her place as a first-class member and also reminding the majority that Christianity cannot be confined to narrow racial and ethnic boundaries. I have seen small children standing on a platform built into the lectern reading Old Testament stories with poise and articulation at a children's Mass.

What Training Is Necessary?

I entered Chicago's Holy Name Cathedral on a Sunday afternoon and encountered a training session for readers. A parishioner who is a seasoned TV announcer was conducting it. Each person would go to the lectern to work on a particular aspect of the skill and be criticized by both trainer and trainees. Very few parishes would have the highly specialized resources of this cathedral parish; neither would they have the demand for such highly skilled readers as one does in a huge cathedral which sees its role as modeling liturgical practice for the archdiocese and speaking to tourists and conventioneers as well as highrise and lowrise dwellers.

The diocese itself could sponsor reader workshops in different regions of the diocese. A professional speech teacher from a nearby educational institution could be engaged in conducting training sessions. The training needs to include more than speech therapy and practice in public speaking. One of the components must be in helping the reader understand the relationship of the reading to the entire liturgy.

To Whom Are the Readers Accountable?

Each parish has its own authority structure with a simple or complicated flow chart. The size of the congregation is one determinant; the other is the history of the pastor and the people as they have accommodated themselves to each other's understanding of authority in the church—pre-Vatican II paternalism or post-Vatican II collegiality.

Ideally, the responsibility for choosing, training, and offering a critique and support to lectors should be in the hands of the liturgy team or the trainer, not the pastor. Collegiality is not developed by throwing every decision back to the pastor.

Questions for Reflection and Discussion

1. How do we help members of the assembly to prepare for the service of the word at home?

2. At what level are the lectors in our parish? How can we help them to move to a deeper level of integration of the word and their lives?

3. Who are our lectors? Do they represent a cross-section of our parish? Do we need to call forth lectors from the elderly, the young, the divorced, the ethnic, the males?

4. How can we provide scriptural background to help readers understand the context and meaning of scripture?

5. Are our readers aware of interpretive skills such as emotional and sense recall? How can we encourage the use of these skills to deepen the assembly's experience of the word proclaimed?

12

PREACHING

How do we respond to the bored, the angry, and the spiritually undernourished who complain about the present state of the homily in the American church? The homily is a tension point in the church today. Prior to Vatican II, homilies were not a critical issue because there were fewer of them. Before the air-conditioned church the pulpit was often vacated in the summer; commentaries on the letters of bishops, annual collections, and the reading of the financial report were easy substitutes. In some dioceses homilies were designed to be instructions on the articles of faith on a three-year cycle that had no reference to the readings, or they may have been moral lessons studded with phrases from the gospel.

It was not until the late sixties that people began to complain, as though homilies were getting worse. A more likely explanation is that in an era of increased literacy and freedom to express dissent, people's expectations of a homily rose without any change in the pulpit. People began to feel that a decently prepared homily was a right. Prior to the revolution of expectations of the sixties we had a cultural Catholicism nourished by Catholic schools and neighborhoods that made the parish a self-contained way of life sealed off from secular society. When the ghetto walls were shattered, we expected the Sunday liturgy focused on the homily to guide us through the complexities of a secular world in a church that was losing confidence in its authoritarian structures. Whether homilies are indeed worse than they were two decades ago or the expectations of people have risen along with permission to express negative feelings, there is an overwhelming conviction that Catholic preaching is in distress.

What do people expect from a Sunday homily? We can presume that a large segment has a built-in switch that turns off their hearing aids as the homily begins. These listeners have learned to sit comfortably as they would in a hospital waiting room until the end. They may have rationalized decades ago that duty and boredom are two sides of one coin. Who said that giving an hour a week to God should be a roller coaster of human feelings? We were told that grace is received by one's presence at Mass.

As Mark Searle writes:

> There is, of course, a certain asceticism involved in going back, Sunday after Sunday, to submit to the inordinate amount of bad preaching that abounds, to put up with the ill-prepared homilies, to suffer paternalistic perorations and clerical authoritarianism and well-intentioned but utterly impractical moralizing. That sort of thing is perhaps what first springs to a lay person's mind when there is talk about the impact of preaching: the sheer flood of inert ideas that washes over our Sunday congregations who are thirsting for the living waters of the Word of God. But there is more to the lay vocation than mere forebearance. The lay listener, like the ordained preacher, has the responsibility of looking for the Word of God which comes, as always, in human guise. God's revelation in the past was no monologue from the clouds, but came borne upon the flowing tide of human experience. Then, as

now, the Word of God was not something one had
simply to listen to, but something one had to listen for:
it involved active human participation in the very
event of revelation and in its gradual assimilation in
faith.

Similarly with the sermon: we have to listen *for*, rather
than just *to*, the Word of God, for it is not to be
supposed that every syllable falling from a preacher's
lips is to be reckoned as inspired of God . . . thus the
first rule of the artful and ascetic listener is this: ignore
the preacher. It may be easier to do this if you close
your eyes. I realize, as a teacher, that this can be very
discouraging to the speaker, but I have not yet person-
ally acquired that degree of perfection where I can see
beyond what holds my gaze; whereas I can, if I close
my eyes, give myself over to very attentive listening for
that which is being spoken behind the words I hear.
But eyes open or eyes shut, the point is to attend *from*
the preacher's words *to* the Word being preached.[1]

The Homily Dramatizes the Struggle

The homily can only dramatize, not enact, the human
struggle. It can only point by story, images, and poetry to
both the gory and ecstatic moments in life. It is a sacred
moment. It makes real the Lord's presence by describing
the human situation in which the Lord is revealing himself.
The Lord's presence can be revealed in homilies that
describe the smell of urine in public housing entrances,
the smile of an infant, the wrinkled faces of the aging. A
gospel story is not simply being repeated. It is being transformed into a lived moment in the history of the community. It is Jesus revealing himself at this family meal of
remembrances.

The homilist is like the patron of a thrift shop picking
up the clothes people threw away. He is holding them up to
the wearer and showing them that they fit either new-style
or rediscovered old-style Christianity. The rags of one person become the promise of redemption for another. The

homily is not a commentary on the gospel, but a kaleido-
scope that picks up electronic waves of present events.
Kasantzakis writes:

> We struggle to make this Spirit visible, to give it a face,
> to encase it in words, in allegories and thoughts and
> incantations, that it may not escape us . . . My God is
> not Almighty. He struggles, for he is in peril every
> moment; he trembles and stumbles in every living
> thing, and he cries out. He is defeated incessantly, but
> rises again, full of blood and earth, to throw himself
> into battle once more.[2]

The Homily Is Not the Centerpiece

We first need to establish common ground on what a homily is for. It is not an after-dinner speech to amuse and
enlighten the guests. Humor can be the spice that makes the
message delightful, and a broad education can offer the
homilist a variety of disciplines to draw from. However,
humor, brilliance, and dramatic flair do not add up to a
good homily. The homily, like liturgical music, is a part of

something larger. It is ancillary, not the centerpiece. It is
meant to engage the assembly in such a way that it is drawn
into the mystery. According to Mark Searle:

> The homily as part of the liturgy itself, is integral to
> our common worship. It is an act of the priestly office
> of Jesus Christ, part of the *sacrum commercium* between
> God and his people in Jesus Christ, through the em-
> powering and uniting Spirit of holiness. It is no mere
> interlude for instruction, no occasion for a speculative
> monologue, but an act of worship shared by the
> speaker and the hearers, an act of magnifying the
> Lord, of recounting his marvelous deeds in the assem-
> bly of his faithful, an act of remembering the God who
> remembers his people.[3]

The homily is the transformation of the human elements of bread and wine becoming the body and blood of
Christ. It is the paschal mystery of Jesus entering the depths
of himself through his suffering and death and being raised
to new life. The transformation is dramatized in the homily
as it depicts the human struggle of the community, which is
expressed in the specific pains and moments of joy in the
community as they are intertwined with the struggles or
beatitudes of Jesus as reflected in the readings. The homily
dramatizes in story form the transformation of the messi-
ness and greatness of our lives, linked with the life of Jesus,
in becoming this new creation that is experienced in faith
throught the eucharistic prayer and communion. The homily is the blood and guts reality of life enveloped in the
mystery and challenged by the promise of God. Bland
homilies that skim the surface of life demean the struggle,
fail to celebrate the presence in human life, and do not lead
us to the awe of mystery.

To Whom Does the Pulpit Belong?

In the chapter on the presider we presumed the faith of the
presiding celebrant and stressed the human development
of the presider as the principal qualification for the presi-

dency of the assembly. We extend this presumption to the homilist. Since the homilist is a storyteller rather than a teacher, the human development of the preacher will be the major focus in communicating God's word. Since storytelling or poetic communication of a vision is at the heart of the homiletic form of communication, we must accept that it requires a rare giftedness. We need to reassess the assumption that every priest and deacon with retraining can give an effective homily. We begin with two contrary assumptions.

In the first place, if a priest has shown no interest in personal or professional renewal in the past fifteen years, we should not invest too much energy in that direction. Second, many priests and deacons of good will are simply not good communicators and are probably not capable of ever becoming good homilists. Ordination may give us the right to preach, but it does not make us effective homilists. I have never heard of a seminarian or deacon candidate turned down for orders because he would not be an effective preacher.

Why not begin from a different starting point by asking the question, "Who in the community can best preach the word of God?" The question focuses on the word being heard by this particular group of people, rather than on the right of the ordained to mount the pulpit. There are several implications for a pastor. He might try convincing a priest, who by a broad parish consensus is not gifted, to let others who are so gifted take his place in the pulpit. Since preaching is at the core of the priestly identity of many priests who are poor preachers, the pastor might be physically assaulted or charged with gross incompetence as an administrator, or worse. However, to continue to permit an incompetent ordained priest and deacon to preach is to accept the "Reverse Caiphas Principle"— "The entire parish should die from not hearing the word of God rather than hurt the feelings of one ungifted priest or deacon."

We offer a few practical suggestions. If the pastor or associate goes on vacation, the pulpit should not be given to priests of other nationalities or cultures who either do not speak English well or do not understand our culture. Likewise, a homily should not be preached in English in a predominantly Hispanic congregation or in any non-English-speaking group. Nor should the pastor take just any priest who is from a local monastery or who volunteers for Sunday liturgies.

But where are we going to get this fresh supply of preachers who are good communicators and who can speak the word of God through the medium of our culture? I build my case on the *Directory for Masses with Children*.[4] There is no reason why one of the adults should not preach a homily to the children after the gospel, especially if the priest has difficulty adapting himself to the mentality of the children. To many this may seem to be contradicted by *Inaestimabile Donum,* issued by the Sacred Congregation for the Sacraments and Divine Worship on April 3, 1980: "The purpose of the homily is to explain to the faithful the word of God proclaimed in the readings and to apply its message to the present. Accordingly the homily is to be given by the priest or the deacon." Since the *Instruction* does not deal with our case of the priest or deacon who is not capable of giving a homily, we lean on the principle of *The Directory for Masses with Children,* namely, find someone who can.

We must understand that our Anglo understanding of church law does not flow from our church tradition. The *Instruction* rightly holds up the norm and the *Directory* allows for the exceptions. This I would call pastoral compassion. The rationale is that the hearing of the word of God by the people is more important than the status of the person preaching.

Lay Preachers

Where will we find substitutes for ungifted priests and deacons? In the pews. Any respectable bookmaker would affirm that with two million Catholics in the archdiocese of Chicago and only 2,500 active priests and deacons, the odds are that we can find an adequate supply of formed Christians who can both understand the scriptures and communicate well. But we don't want the chaos of the charismatics of Corinth, that is, gifted people using their gifts destructively because there is no order. The West German bishops found a way. In 1973 they were given a four-year permission to set up a system for the certification of lay preachers. This grant was renewed for four more years in 1977.

In the Middle Ages preaching was in disarray, probably worse than today. The people were saved by the Franciscan and other lay movements. Our church has more flexibility than we might think.

In 1978 the Canon Law Society of America voted to ask the American bishops to seek permission from Rome to permit "qualified non-ordained members of the church to preach under certain circumstances." Father James Provost comments on the resolution:

> Preaching by the clergy may be a source of irritation in the Christian community already. But unqualified or inopportune preaching by lay persons can be an even more abrasive event. Safeguards are needed to protect congregations from the tyranny of unprepared speakers; to promote the training and appropriate involvement of lay persons in witnessing their faith and the teachings of the church; to assert the rights and responsibilities of pastors who are charged with providing adequate preaching for the community . . . the present situation lacks these safeguards. Moreover, in the light of the positive reevaluation of the role of lay persons in the church since the Second Vatican Council, the current restrictions appear too severe and in practice are largely unenforceable in many local areas.

> The resolution also noted that a number of situations exist under current church norms where the lay people are permitted to "preach" in the broad sense of the term. Lectors are commissioned by the bishops to "instruct children and adults in the faith." Lay leaders or commentators may make various comments within the liturgy. Even "homilies" by lay persons are already permitted in specialized circumstances when

there is no priest or deacon, such as at the exposition of the blessed sacrament or at celebrations of the word . . . .

The canon lawyers suggest that the principles in these other situations can be used to expand the occasions for lay preaching under serious pressing pastoral conditions. These include utilizing the language, cultural and professional skills of lay persons when local clergy are not able to relate effectively with minority groups or certain age groups. Lay persons are taking an increasingly important role in evangelization. Occasional lay preaching within the context of the liturgy may increase the general awareness of this evangelization.[5]

Qualities of a Good Homily

We present two views on preaching, the first from a young pastor, Robert McLaughlin:

It's my suspicion that good sermons and sensitive, understanding priests are very closely related. The good homilist will reflect that he has *listened to and understood his people*. His choice of topic, his word choice, his examples will all reflect that he has heard from their experience as well as what he knows from his own. Where possible he will identify with them in their struggles so that people will nod their heads and say "Yes, that's what I feel. He knows what it's like." Only when people feel understood are they open to growth. Like Solomon we should pray that we may have "an understanding heart."

Just as he listens to his people, the homilist will listen to the word of God; he will listen to the Spirit groaning within him. In other words, the effective homilist will be a person who prays, who takes time to reflect on the scriptures. It's only when we have spent time in prayerful reflection that the word "becomes like fire burning in my heart."

It is my impression that the good homilist will be a credible person. Somehow our lives have to reflect that we believe what we say. Not that we are perfect—but that we continue to struggle, to be open. The other aspect of credibility is that we *never* speak what we don't believe.

Witness what has happened to the church's teaching on sexual ethics! Witness how—in the United States—we ring hollow when we talk about social justice. People generally do not believe what we say because we do not give evidence that we know what we are talking about or that we really believe what we say. When people no longer believe what we say, our effectiveness as homilists is shattered.

I think that a good homily has to be *hopeful*. We have confidence that we and others can change. This will enable us to keep a sense of humor about how things are and a willingness to confront what needs to be confronted. Being hopeful will also give us the energy we need to work hard in the preparation of homilies. When we give up on our people, it's very hard to motivate ourselves to spend the time and energy that are needed to prepare a good homily.

What are the resources that I find helpful? The *Jerome Biblical Commentary* is by far the most important book that I use. I also like the *Anchor Bible Notes and Commentaries*. In addition, I find authors like Irma Bombeck and Sam Levinson helpful because they see the humor in the human condition.

In some ways the greatest resources I have are the counseling sessions, the parties in the parish, and the time spent in front of church on Sunday morning. By listening in these circumstances, not only do I learn what people's real feelings and issues are, but I try also to listen to the words that *they* use to express themselves so that when I preach I can reflect their feelings in their language.[6]

Larry Ragan, a lay professor, writer, and lecturer on communications, has spent decades sitting in front of the pulpil silently dialoguing with the preacher.

> The priest should know the congregation sitting in front of him, not the one that used to sit in the same seats. The world has changed; people have changed. On Labor Day weekend last year I heard a priest discuss how hard the men of the parish worked. They deserved, he said, peace and quiet in the home, not to mention a good dinner when they got there. Ye gods, I asked myself, where has he been? There were as many women workers in the parish as there were men, but he talked as if he were living at the turn of the century and the men were all returning from the steel mills and coal mines as their women were waiting at the doors, drying their hands in their aprons.

> The priest should resist speaking about his childhood or his family. He should especially avoid doing so if he is past fifty, because the chances are that his family is—or was—different from my family. True (to those in their fifties), he may have said family prayers. He also may have come from a family of ten children, three others of whom are either nuns or priests. That family has little relevance to the people in the congregation today. Most of them don't understand it. The young people laugh at it. Ten children, you say? Ten? And you knelt on the living room floor and said the rosary? You did? Sure you did, but hide that fact as you would a sinful past. It doesn't communicate to us in the pews.

> Read vigorously, read widely, read constantly, and quote often from what you read. The priest should not read what other priests have written unless they are among the great. It would be much better if he read some poetry, some contemporary novels, a bit of sociology, even the *New York Times*. He should relate his reading to his life and to ours. In a life of listening to sermons, I recall only a handful of literary allusions

priests have made. I still remember the last. It was from Silone's *Bread and Wine*. That was ten years ago. I have not heard one since.

The priest should not worry how he looks or sounds as he stands in the pulpit. That's why the suggestion to establish videotaped training is pointless. Such training does little good. The speaker is effective only when he has something to say, when his words will touch the listener. The emphasis on pronunciation, gesture, facial expression, and all the rest merely distracts the speaker from the essentials, that is, the ideas embodied in the words he uses, however haltingly. The timbre of the voice and the drama of the gesture mean little when the ideas are hackneyed, the sentiments soft-headed, and the advice unrealistic. Our problem in the pews is not that we cannot hear the words but rather that we can hear them too well.[7]

Prophetic Preaching

Scriptural preaching that stays close to the readings and liturgical homilies that lead us to worship can fail to be adequately prophetic. Homilies must challenge as well as comfort, must ask people to do the impossible and repugnant as well as the pleasing.

Although I have been preaching homilies that touch on social issues for forty years, I find it continually to be a greater challenge. I probably put more time into the preparation of the Sunday homily commemorating the death of Oscar Romero than into any talk I have given on race, welfare, housing, or Vietnam. As our political and economic structures evolve, the issues become more complicated. But there is also a change in me; I am trying to be more sensitive to the people who make a different political and economic analysis than I, as well as to those who have their own understanding of church, prayer, and morality.

I have never accepted the criticism that a homily should not be political. Christianity has been politicized since the day Jesus told off the Pharisees and kicked over the money tables. After a homily on Vietnam a parishioner told me that I should not speak on political issues. "You mean I should not speak on abortion or federal aid to Catholic schools?" "That's different," she responded. Pope John Paul II had political overtones to his homilies in Mexico, Poland, Brazil, and at the Washington Mall.

While I have no pangs of guilt for using the pulpit to help bring to birth the Medicare legislation fought by the A.M.A. as "socialized medicine," I have become more respectful of the people in front of me today. If I talk about Romero's death, I must envision both the pacifists and militants in the congregation. They believe in the same Jesus and submit themselves to the judgment of his gospel. My goal is to challenge both of them at the same time. I fantasize each shaking hands with me after Mass and saying, "I am not sure I can buy what you are asking, but you may have a point. I'll pray about it."

It takes a long time to prepare talks with both in mind. I must speak to the deepest common vein of humanity in both of them. In the situation that Romero's death symbolizes there is a sinfulness that involves me as well as them. The challenge is for me to name it. How do I speak to the common sinfulness in this and in other social situations and point to the path that leads to redemption? I must find a language for talking about it that speaks to people's daily experience. It is not a place for a lecture or information, but rather for moving people to give a gospel response to an event that touches their lives.

The easiest path is to forget it all and just talk Sunday after Sunday about better communications in our personal relationships by getting in touch with our true feelings. It is relatively easy to identify the Lord's presence and absence in our personal encounters. You tell the stories of when it happened and when it didn't. This is what the people clamor for.

But not to engage our congregation through homilies in social issues is to bless the *status quo* and not acknowledge our sinfulness. It is to say that politics, economics, and social life are either beyond redemption or have been redeemed.

To eliminate this dimension of preaching is to emasculate the gospel, to refuse to accept the craziness of Christ in holding up the beatitudes as norm for public as well as private behavior.

I acknowledge that the people in front of me on Sunday have not come for this message. They bring their woundedness and hope to be touched by my healing words. In front of me is the spouse of an active alcoholic, the parent of an addicted son or daughter, couples giving their marriage a last chance, and people for whom the last chance has not worked. In front of me are people who feel neglected because of age, people mourning from a recent death in the family, the guilt-ridden person still suffering after having received the Lord's forgiveness for being an adulterer. The young and old are crying for a word that will be a saving word, a crumb or crust that may become the bread of life.

I listen to myself talking back to the people in front of me who confront me with their life struggles:

> Yes, I hear you. I am close to tears. Your every ache and pain is mine, but I am going to disappoint you today. I will respond to your cries next Sunday. Today I want to talk about the wounds of the people in El Salvador. I don't understand all the political nuances of the situation, but I do ask you to bear your pain as Archbishop Romero bore the pain of his people. If you can participate in his suffering, it might make your own pain less acute. Our pains and his pain together are the "filling up of those things wanting in the Body of Christ."

The prophetic homily must be the exception. The ordinary Sunday fare describes where the shoe pinches, names the pains and aches along with the joys of the simple things of life. The genius is in the mix of the prophetic and the pedestrian. An overdose of prophecy tells the people that you are only interested in your causes and do not care about their experiences. To fail to include the prophetic and settle for psychology, scripture, and theology, if one is learned, or to tell stories of human life without ever putting them into the context of the entire family, is to emasculate the gospel.

Questions for Reflection and Discussion

1. What do we expect from a Sunday homily? Have these expectations ever been communicated directly to the homilists?

2. What is the assembly's role in the preaching experience?

3. Following the precedent set in the *Directory for Masses with Children,* have we considered who else in our parish could best preach the word of God?

4. Do we ever hear any prophetic preaching? How can this be encouraged in our homilists?

5. How are parish homilies formed? Do parishioners have a significant part either in the formation or the feedback? Should such a process be set up?

13

BREAKING OF THE BREAD I

I received word that an elderly woman to whom I bring communion was in Chicago's Mercy Hospital. It was a ten-mile drive to the hospital. We had a pleasant visit, exchanging bits of information and small talk and ending with prayer. The next day she called a parish deacon and asked him to bring her communion. I was puzzled. Mercy Hospital brings communion to its patients daily at the patient's convenience. It never occurred to me that she would want communion from a parish minister. On reflection it seems that she may have had a more authentic understanding of the eucharist than I had. Communion is the table of the Lord, a fellowship and sisterhood of believers. A few days in the hospital were not enough for her to become a member of the Mercy community of believers who share the one bread and drink from the same cup. The deacon was able to compensate for my failure to link her to the St. Victor community through the bread from St. Victor's holy meal.

Regina Kuehn

Robert Warner was a fulltime pastoral associate at St. James Parish, which had responsibility for pastoral ministry to Catholic patients at Michael Reese Hospital. Before giving them the bread to eat, he told them that this bread was from the Mass at which he participated and that the people of St. James were praying that morning for those who would receive communion from this table. People would proceed to confess their sins. He tried to interrupt their litany to tell them he was not a priest and would arrange for the priest to come. The patients would not be interrupted. The message seemed to be that, ordained or not, you are the church of "my father's holy faith." The fact that it was a layman who linked them to the holy table was not as significant as the reality of sharing vicariously in the assembly of St. James.

One of St. Victor's eucharistic ministers took a busman's holiday and went to Mass at the cathedral. He came back astonished that three priests would come from the sacristy at communion time to distribute communion. He had only experienced St. Victor's, where the communion ministers all participate in the assembly at which they minister the eucharist. It is the community ministering to itself.

The parishioner registered astonishment at the disruption to the flow of the liturgy by priests filing out in lockstep at communion time to give out communion at a Mass at which they had not sung, prayed, or listened to the word of God. Unlike the presider, they were interlopers or functionaries, not participants. This would only be felt by a parishioner who sees the eucharist as a total action, not as a sacramental dispensary. Like the patients in the hospital, he had an intuition that the sacraments are related to an assembly and that the communicant and the one ministering communion are linked in the same assembly, where they have prayed together in this celebration. The question is not whether the Lord is present in the sacrament being received, but whether the sacrament is a believable sign of communion with the assembly, which is a microcosm of the human family.

The early Christians described the eucharist as the breaking of the bread, a table fellowship of believers. The New Testament has been described as a book of table manners. The guest without a wedding garment at the marriage banquet is probably the most dramatic gospel illustration of bad manners. Eucharistic ministers waiting in the sacristy for their turn to come on stage diminish the table as the sign of the heavenly banquet. Such behavior violates New Testament etiquette.

I explained to our parishioner that what he saw at the cathedral was legally correct and that the people in charge of cathedral and papal liturgies have a need to stick to the letter of the law lest they encourage other parishes to bend the law to fit their theology. In a 1973 papal decree, permission for eucharistic ministers was granted, not with the New Testament reasoning or to appease lay people who want a greater share in the assembly, but for pragmatic reasons. "Provision must be made," wrote Pope Paul VI, "lest reception of communion become impossible or difficult because of insufficient ministers."

The American bishops in typical American pragmatic style explained the reason for the monumental shift. Lay ministers are necessary

> ... When there is a large number of regular communicants at the parochial liturgy and a shortage of ordinary ministers to assist the president of the assembly in the distribution of the eucharist. A shortage of eucharistic ministers, in such a case, caused the communion rite to be out of proportion to the total celebration. The goal is not, however, to shorten or have more efficient Masses, but to give them their proper value and to avoid the rush it takes to distribute communion to everyone present. [1]

While the law is clear, there is a wide diversity of practice because of an equally wide spectrum of theological understandings of the most elementary sacraments of baptism and eucharist. While Vatican II was a historic moment in summarizing the theological development of the past five hundred years, it opened doors and windows to further development not foreseen by the council. When there is a cultural and theological development not accompanied by a change in the law, we develop a rationale until the law is updated. We make accommodations that broaden the concept and practice without breaking the law. Therefore, in the United States we have in practice reinterpreted "the shortage of available priests." The clerical staff feels that except for the Mass they celebrate, they should be emotionally available for greeting the people before and after each Mass, and attending to people who cannot make appointments other than Sunday morning, rather than racing to the sacristy at the Lamb of God to toss on the vestments and shift gears to be spiritually and emotionally available to each communicant at every Mass. (In the era when greeting people before and after Mass was not a pastoral value, the pastor might spend Sunday morning making tracks from the counting room to the sacristy, ministering to the counters and communicants alternately.)

Only the priest knows the dulling effect on his spiritual life of being burnt out from the treadmill from the Sunday paper to the sacristy. The burnout comes not from the physical effort, but from the psychological and spiritual weariness of being a spiritual robot dispensing sacraments without human interchange.

The lay ministers of the eucharist have a different experience than the holy chore of priest distributors. "I have always loved the eucharist without understanding it," was the first response of Mary Cunnea of Ford City when I asked her how she came to be a eucharistic minister. "When I was approached by Dolly, I agreed. After I started, I wanted to quit. I was physically shaking, but I was encouraged to continue. Now I am one of the trainers. When I am giving out communion I have a great sense we are all in this together. It is a community prayer. I feel the presence of God in the middle of it. Previously my prayer was private—God and me."

We are caught in both the rapids and the backwaters of post-Vatican II renewal and regression. The push and pull in opposite directions is in the same assembly, same rectory, and same diocese. The static or regressive side sees the sacraments yielding grace simply by following the ritual or script without deviation or imagination. Linked to this is a view of priesthood that sees the priest as the chief dispenser of grace. In the revolutionary document of Vatican II on the church we see the same forward and backward pushes and pulls. It makes no specific reference to lay people being ministers. It confines the word to priests by using "sacred ministers" and "sacred pastors." The sacred ministry of the priest is contrasted with the faithful "who lend their cooperative assistance."

On the opposite side of the street we find a growing segment of the church talking about the assembly as the priesthood of 1 Peter 2.5. This text is used as a basis for the eucharistic minister as a sacred minister whose role comes from baptism rather than from a trickle-down from the sacrament of priesthood. After the decree of 1973 allowing hands that were not anointed in the sacrament of holy orders to minister the bread and the cup, we allowed the entire assembly to receive the bread in their hands because of their baptism. The *general instruction* allowed the auxiliary minister to assist the priest in the breaking of bread, the focal symbol of the entire eucharist. While these decrees act as equalizers, they do not wipe out priesthood. The priest's role becomes more focused.

What does this do to the priest as the church moves with ambiguity from a sanctuary or hierarchical view of ministry to an assembly-centered community of worship? He can find authority figures and documents to back up whatever way he swings. He may need to take a stand after taking psychological inventory and say, "If the layman takes over what is exclusively mine, who am I?" He may fear the consequences of veering to the left lest he lose his needed emotional support from the right. When we take away the intellectual or theological wrappings, we may see that the ego needs of the priest is the issue that demands our response of ministering to the minister.

Selection

Since Catholics center their identity around the eucharist, we must expect strong feelings to emerge in the selection of auxiliary ministers. Pope Paul VI has given us excellent guidelines:

> The person who has been appointed . . . must be duly instructed and should distinguish himself or herself by Christian life, faith, and morals, striving to be worthy of this great office, cultivating devotion to the holy eucharist and acting as an example to the other faithful by the piety and reverence for this most holy sacrament of the altar. Let no one be chosen whose selection may cause scandal among the faithful.[2]

"Who do you ask to be ministers?" Mary Cunnea of Ford City replied, "In reaching out to invite ministers we look for people who love the liturgy and the eucharist. It takes people who like to relate on a one-to-one basis, rather than a person who projects herself as a reader or who likes to preach."

I asked Bob Quinn of St. Victor how he became a eucharistic minister. "It must have happened to me a half-dozen times. A staff person or a eucharistic minister would come up to me and say, 'We are short one minister. Are you a eucharistic minister?' So I figured I should volunteer." Apparently the assembly was telling him something. In theological or biblical language it is labeled "the call." He sees himself as sharing his faith. On his part he opens himself to the communicant with a smile and eye contact. With some people he finds that there is no openness to a human encounter, but with the majority he finds himself nourished by the faith of the people who are open to his expression of faith. He is still learning. "I find the ushers helpful in identifying people who cannot get in line, but I also keep an eye open for someone they may miss."

Some parishioners will respond when asked, "Lord, I am not worthy." Others who feel that others were asked in preference to themselves may respond, "Lord, how could they pick such an unworthy person as Mary Jones?"

The process of selection must involve the entire parish, but need not be an election. Names need to be solicited through the bulletin or pulpit announcements and forwarded to the designated staff member. The staff must agree on the selection process. The names of nominees should not be published, so that, if necessary, a name can be withdrawn for reasons that would embarrass the nominee. Selection should be based on many considerations in an effort to present a representative group inclusive of sexes, ages, races, nationalities, economic statuses, and the handicapped. An effort should be made to provide as many parish role models as possible. The pastor has the final responsibility for the selection of the candidates.

Training

Dioceses may provide training sessions for their eucharistic ministers. The obvious advantage is their ability to gather highly skilled trainers and theologians in the area. The parish by definition has limited access to high-powered and expensive resources. The advantages of local training sessions, besides limiting transportation problems, are the faith-sharing and community development that can take place if it is a parish undertaking.

At Ford City two laywomen, Mary Cunnea and Bev Sigler, are trainers and coordinators of the eucharistic ministers, who in turn report to the staff liturgist, Dolly Sokol. There are two sessions for the annual training of new ministers. In the first session the trainers present a history of the eucharist. With their theological understanding of the eucharist gleaned from Tad Guzie's book *Jesus and the Eucharist*,[3] they engage the group in a discussion on the theology of eucharist. The eucharistic ministers are the foremost communicators of the theology of assembly by who they are, how they understand their role in the assembly, and the way they minister. Without carefully prepared training sessions they may simply imitate the caricatured cleric in dispensing sacraments, perpetuating a new clericalism in lay garb. It is the gestures of the minister, rather than the printed word or the homily, that will be most effective in shaping the community in a new understanding of the eucharist that speaks to the breaking of the bread and the sharing of the holy meal as the Lord has commanded us. This is done with a slide presentation and commentary.

A training session is necessary for many reasons. 1) There is need to let the trainees know how special they are, as well as the holiness of the office itself. 2) The trainee needs to find out how she or he fits into the evolving theology and ritual of the eucharist. 3) There is a need for a hands-on practice session. 4) The new ministers need the support of one another that comes from sharing the new experiences. 5) Time is needed to sort out and match the scheduling needs of the parish with the commitments of the parishioner. 6) Beginnings need to be celebrated.[2]

The second part of the first session at Ford City is a hands-on-practice. Trainees become acquainted with the vessels and later practice with each other. Questions about movement to the altar and position at altar, assisting in the fraction rite, and the movement to and from the altar are rehearsed. The session ends with a prayer service that concludes with the sharing of many kinds of bread and drinking grape juice from goblets.

All eucharistic ministers are invited to the second session. It begins with music that leads to centering prayer, which is an introduction to a sharing session where people are able to talk about what the eucharist meant to them as children and how they have grown to their present adult understanding. In this way they are able to articulate, not Tad Guzie's theology, but their own, which is in development and confirmed by the group. The second session is the annual renewal and spiritual development session for veteran ministers as well as the new.

The trainers do the scheduling of ministers of the eucharist and are able to criticize beginning ministries. The ministers are appointed for a year with an option to renew. The annual meeting with the new ministers is a marking point for them to review and renew their commitment.

Since the auxiliary minister is a public person in the church, it seems that a public acknowledgment needs to be made. While Ford City does this on Commitment Sunday when they are a part of a larger group, each parish needs to design the service to respond to their own understanding of public ministry and their particular needs.

Questions for Reflection and Discussion

1. What are the connections between the ministry of the eucharist and the ministry of greeter or welcomer? How can these characteristics become more a part of the eucharistic minister?

2. What qualities does a truly "eucharistic" minister need?

3. What are the differences between a eucharistic minister at Mass and a eucharistic minister to the sick? Are different gifts needed?

4. Why is it integral to the liturgy that all ministers, including eucharistic ministers, participate in the entire Mass?

5. How can we prevent the eucharistic ministry from becoming hierarchical or quasi-clerical? If it becomes this, what happens to the other ministries, including the ministry of the assembly?

6. Why is it important for eucharistic ministers to be familiar with the current theology of the eucharist?

14

BREAKING OF THE BREAD II

I was sitting next to a state senator at a New Year's party at Chicago's Greek Islands. I had met her a number of times previously, admired her for political skills, her brilliance as a law professor, and her advocacy of liberal causes, but I always said to myself, "What is she really like?" The answer came when she pointed to an elderly man sitting alone in the restaurant and said to me, "Do you see that man over there by himself?" I probably had, but now I was being commissioned to go and sit with the man. He was soon in tears telling me his story of loneliness, of how his sons had not invited him to their homes, and showing me pictures of his grandchildren. I invited him to our table. It was at the Greek Islands in the breaking of the New Year's bread that I came to know the state senator.

Thomas Campbell, former President of Chicago Theological Seminary, told how as a young minister in a small town he gave well-prepared and well-delivered sermons, and offered his pastoral services with all the skills and enthusiasm of a beginner. But he did not feel that he was accepted by the community. The turn-around came when an elderly man called and asked him if he could get help in moving. He responded by carrying the man's bed across town on the roof of his car. This was the sign the parishioners were waiting for. In the carrying of the bed they came to know him and warmly accept him. It is an Emmaus story. The moment of recognition came in the carrying of the bed rather than in the breaking of the bread.

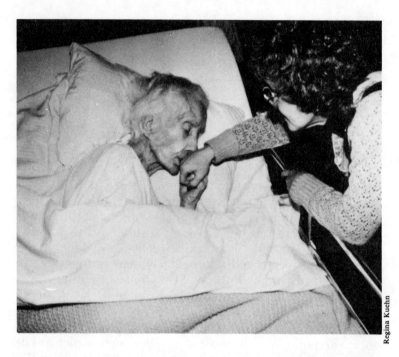

Regina Kuehn

The Emmaus story is an elemental Christian symbol that has unlimited possibilities for disclosure of the good news in human events. The event begins with two men having a friendly conversation as they walked. They were open enough to a stranger to include him in their journey, but not open enough to recognize that it was the Lord. The stranger injects himself into the conversation by bluntly asking, "What matters are you discussing as you walk along?" The depressing story is repeated to the stranger as bad news. It was a story of false expectations and shattered dreams. The stranger chides them with his opener, "You foolish men," for their failure to take the scriptures seriously. It was another opportunity for them to recognize that it was this stranger about whom the scriptures were talking. They were still blinded to his real presence.

The turning point comes when, as he feigns going on his way, "they pressed him to stay with them." The moment of disclosure comes quickly. "Now while he was with them at table, he took the bread and said the blessing; then he broke it and handed it to them. And their eyes were opened and they recognized him. . . ."

Like every scripture story the emergents are unlimited. I offer a few. The breaking of bread was a community meal setting, but it was what they brought to the restaurant that made the disclosure possible, namely, their openness to the stranger. They were willing to share their depression with him but, more important, they invited him to their table. It was only when they found him in the breaking of the bread that they were able to reflect on their feelings on the road. "Did not our hearts burn within us as he talked to us on the road and explained the scriptures to us?" They understood Kirkegaard's one-liner, "We live life forward and understand it backwards."

The emerging thought for those of us who wish to make liturgies real is that there is something more to good liturgies than good presiding, lectoring, preaching, drama, art, and ministering the eucharist. It is how the individuals in the assembly relate to others on the way, that is, at home, work, play, and politics. Good liturgies hinge on our hospitality in receiving strangers, new ideas, and being open to new ways of doing familiar things. The eucharistic ministers can dramatize the breaking of the bread by taking a loaf of bread and in visible fashion dramatically breaking it into pieces small enough to be eaten, but their eyes may not be opened. It will be another liturgical gimmick unless they are bringing lives broken for others to the assembly's sharing rite. We cannot grasp the symbolism of the liturgical breaking of the bread until we allow ourselves to be bread for others.

The two incidents that introduced this chapter are simply stories of breaking bread that anyone can understand—the woman who has a sensitive eye for the elderly man eating by himself on New Year's eve; the minister carrying the old man's bed on the roof of his car.

Hospitality and the breaking of the bread cannot be separated from life. The connection is dramatized on Sunday mornings by the coffee urns in the church hall and rectory, an American sign of table welcome. In these parishes the facilities are opened for people to linger on the premises to let the conversations stimulated by community prayer continue as the disciples did with the stranger on the Emmaus road and restaurant. The thrust of the eucharist can be lost if one attempts to carry it in a hermetically sealed personhood from church to parking lot. The mingling after the liturgy can be as significant as the initial greeting period before the liturgy.

Hospitality American-style is done through committees that organize and assign responsibilities so that sharing and caring have maximum coverage and effectiveness. The hospitality that has its center point at the eucharistic table from which the caring flows and to which it returns needs to be organized so that chance encounters can be expanded in ever-widening circles to reach everyone with particular needs. Without organization there would be a large segment of needy persons and areas of concern that would fall between the cracks.

A parish must set up its caring priorities. It would seem that at the top of the list would be nursing homes, the sick and elderly who have no visitors, the poor and the unemployed. The St. Victor hospital and nursing visitation ministry team meets the challenges of the terminally ill, the parishioners who want to link their sufferings with the parish community during their stay in the hospital. However, the nursing homes present their own unique challenge. Pat, Therese, Charlotte, Rita, and Sister Maura sit with people who are slipping out of rationality into senility. These women know how to communicate through touch and in the interaction let the love of Christ diffuse itself in the elderly. The stench of nursing homes and grossly inadequate care due to profit-hungry owners have taught these gentle women to confront the managers as advocates of the helpless.

The stresses and strains of urban life propelled by our consumer society are reflected in family disorganization, leaving a trail of human wreckage, child abuse, spouse beating, and addictive behavior. A eucharistic community needs to be in touch with the resources of the community, to help these hurting people make contact with the people who have the special skills needed to turn the disruptive behavior to wholesome and constructive ways of living. St. Victor Parish has been able to go beyond the referral role and establish an outreach team that is available with a simple phone call to families that are suffering from the ravages of addiction. Two staff members with professional training are joined by ten other parishioners who through in-service training are able to act as paraprofessionals. The parish facilities are also available to Alcoholics Anonymous and Alateen.

St. Victor's Well is for the divorced, but is not an organization to keep them together as a fraternity or sorority. It is a service for the newly divorced wherein they can experience, week after week, the healing ministry of people as they pass through the anger and the grief of their divorce to the healing stance of reconciliation. The ministers of the Well are people who have suffered the pain of divorce and who are capable of using their own woundedness as their chief instrument of ministry. The bread that is broken in our liturgies is a symbol that has the possibilities of enlarging the capability of the addicted and the alienated from the church and society.

When Victor Care resettled a Vietnamese family—renting and furnishing the apartment, filling its cupboards and refrigerator—the family was invited to each assembly on successive Sundays to be officially welcomed to the eucharistic community. The gifts of parishioners to Victor Care family tables become consecrated and made sacred by the sharing that extends from one family table to another and actualizes our Sunday breaking of the bread.

The eucharistic table symbolizes the table of the human family. The bread of life is meant to nourish and bring together in a communion of love the entire human race. Church assemblies of all denominations seem to restrict table fellowship to people of the same race, class, and nationality or ethnic origin. Since our neighborhoods are stratified, the membership of our churches tends to reflect the stereotypes reflected in the housing patterns.

Without a catalytic agent the neighborhoods become enclaves that reinforce individualistic values and see people of other classes and races as nonpeople or enemies. Without raising their voices to utter prophetic words, churches have been guilty of perpetuating the divisiveness that makes "Peace on Earth" the sentimental song of the angels, unrelated to real life. The breaking of the bread is the symbol that calls all of us to expand our worldview and see one another across the historic chasms that divide us.

Why do our Sunday eucharistic assemblies have so little effect upon our lives? Why after the thousands of times we have repeated the ritual are we still turned inward and have little concern with people beyond our kind and class? Father Robert Hovda, in a lecture at the Chicago Liturgy Week, said that we have domesticated the eucharist because we have domesticated the bible. We have muted the prophetic rage of our biblical heritage.

We are remiss in relating "Whatsoever you do to the least of my brethren" to the two-thirds of the world who go to bed hungry. We have difficulty in relating "Blessed are the peacemakers" to our military-industrial complex, which makes us merchants of death through the manufacturing, selling, and storing of weapons capable of destroying the planet. We restrict the meaning of the bread of life to our immediate concerns, family, and friends. Our "privatization" of the eucharist and our limited understanding of the human family is criticized by a Sri Lankan:

The understanding concerning the eucharist has not always been the same throughout these centuries in the different lands and among conflicting social classes. In fact the meaning of the eucharist has been altered by the social pressures. There have been serious distortions in its meaning. Whereas it began with the sacrifice of self for the liberation of others, it has for long been a means of enslavement and domestication of believers.

The eucharist has always remained central to Christianity; but it has been adjusted to suit the needs of the dominant groups in the churches. There has been a social conditioning of the eucharist. This is only one aspect of the overall subordination of the Christian religion to the powers that be in society . . . Feudalism, capitalism, colonialism, racism, and sexism have all tended to make the eucharist conform to their values and priorities . . . The words of the eucharist have been maintained but their meaning has been evacuated, substituted, or distorted. The extent to which even the core rites of a religion can thus be subjected to serve the ruling elites is not surprising but frightening.[1]

Yet hope abounds. In the eighties a significant number of American bishops have issued pastorals on peace, race, the poor, and sexism. The bishops of Seattle, Washington, and Amarillo, Texas, have called for prophetic countercultural actions such as withholding taxes and severing employment with nuclear weapons factories. Such actions may ultimately divide us as a community in the way the Lord describes, mother against mother-in-law. The bread as the sign of unity that makes us one will take us to depths of meaning that it never had before. The assembly that has faced these global concerns and accepted the hard choices they imply will not be apathetic when it gathers around the altar with people searching themselves as they agonize over difficult choices. The response will be perceived in the vivaciousness of the singing.

The pastoral letters of our bishops on social issues will be straws in the wind until our liturgy planning committee translates the parish response into the ritual so that through the breaking of the bread we will be able to see the face of the Lord in our dedication to disarmament, our acceptance of the challenge to feed the world, our commitment to the life of the unborn, and our concern for preserving our environment.

In the pastoral letter of the Roman Catholic bishops of Appalachia, *This Land Is Home To Me,* we have the dream or vision of what we are called to be by the breaking of the bread:

> Dear sisters and brothers, we urge all of you not to stop living, to be a part of the rebirth of utopias. . . . For it is the weak things of this world, which seem like folly, that the Spirit takes up and makes its own. . . . The dream of simplicity and of justice, like so many other repressed visions, is, we believe, the voice of the Lord among us. In taking them up, hopefully the Church might once again be known as
>
> - a center of the Spirit
> - a place where poetry dares to speak
> - where song reigns unchallenged
> - where art flourishes
> - where nature is welcome
> - where little people and little needs come first
> - where justice speaks loudly
> - where in a wilderness of idolatrous destruction, the great voice of God still cries out for Life.
>
> Our Sunday Liturgy is a call to live.[2]

In this chapter we have been criticizing our liturgies as reflections of the gospel. The Emmaus story challenges us to look at our liturgies to see if they capture an Emmaus hospitality in our parish, church, home, neighborhood, and workplace. Our reflections on the judgment scene of Matthew 25 challenge us to look at our eucharists as the celebration of our response to the hungry, the alienated, the disenfranchised, and a nuclear weapons mentality that threatens our survival as a race. We need to listen again to the words of Jesus in promising us the eucharist.

> I am the bread of life . . .
> For my flesh is real food
> And my blood is real drink . . .
> I am the living bread that has come down from heaven
> Anyone who eats this bread will live for ever
> and the bread that I shall give
> is my flesh for the life of the world (John 6:35:51–56).

Bread in John's gospel is a metaphor for self-giving. The bread and the cup are symbols of self-donation, not giving from our abundance as we do when we use our income tax to write off our gifts, but giving of the substance of ourselves from our very need. In the early church there was no need to talk about this, since it was dramatized by the people of the Way who left the table of the Lord to be thrown to the lions.

The prophets disparaged feasts and assemblies, the noise of hymns, burnt offerings and sacrifices, indeed prayer itself, when separated from the cries of the poor, the suffering of the oppressed. Our aim in this book is to make our liturgies vehicles for assemblies that themselves become, week by week, transformed into the bread of life. Thus through the eucharist members become bread for the world.

The test of a good liturgy is not the "high" or the good feeling that it gives us, but the challenge we experience in being called to give our lives as bits of bread, piece by piece, for the life of the world.

Martin Luther King, Jr. dreamed the impossible dream that all of us might be one. It was not the dreams he had at night, but the dream he faced every waking moment, that made his life, death, and our memory of him holy bread, the bread that had its final consecration on the motel balcony in Memphis.

A documentary, *Roses in December,* told the story of Jean Donovan, who was murdered in El Salvador. She had lived a full life as a child, student, professional, and lover, but she wanted to give more. She was advised by all not to return after a vacation because the killings were escalating. As she listened to those who loved her she saw the faces of the refugee children whom she left. She chose to be bread for them. In giving her life for them she became bread for everyone who watched the documentary or heard the story. Daily martyrdom, not simply professionalism, is the final test of our liturgies. However, we want to do our liturgies as ritual well so that the assembly might individually and collectively be bread for the world.

Questions for Reflection and Discussion

1. How do I "break bread" in my daily life?

2. How do we as a parish community "break bread" outside of Mass?

3. Does our parish have outreach programs to touch the sick, elderly and homebound? the unemployed? the alienated? the refugee? the chemically dependent? If not, do we know where community resources are available and how to put people in touch?

4. Do I/Does our parish see justice as a constitutive element of being a Christian in the world? Is there any ongoing education/ action for social justice? Do our liturgies ever reflect on justice issues?

5. Do our liturgies challenge us to be bread for the world?

NOTES
AND
SUGGESTED READINGS

Preface

Note

1. Dennis Geaney, O.S.A., "Liturgy and Life," *Orate Frates,* January 1951.

Chapter 1

For Further Reading

Hoffman, Rabbi. *The Assembly.* Washington, D.C.: Federation of Diocesan Liturgical Commissions, 1981 (cassette of the major address at the 1981 F.D.L.C. Convention).

Walsh, Eugene A., S.S. *The Ministry of the Celebrating Community.* Glendale, Arizona: Pastoral Arts Associates of North America, 1977.

Chapter 2

Notes

1. Andrew M. Greeley, *The Young Catholic Family* (Chicago: Thomas More Press, 1980), ch. 4.

2. Dennis J. Geaney, O.S.A., *Living With Sorrow* (Chicago: Thomas More Press, 1977).

3. Ira Progoff, *The White Robed Monk* (New York: Dialogue House, 1972).

4. Ralph A. Keifer, "A Spirituality of Mystery," *Spirituality Today*, June 1981, p. 105.

5. Sam Keen, *To a Dancing God* (New York: Harper and Row, 1970), p. 159.

6. Charles Davis, "Liturgy Is Not What You Make It," *U.S. Catholic*, October 1976, p. 25. Excerpted with permission from U.S. Catholic, published by Claretian Publications, 221 W. Madison St., Chicago, Ill. 60606.

For Further Reading

Parish Ministry. New York: Parish Project (bimonthly newsletter).

Untener, Kenneth E. *Sunday Liturgy Can Be Better.* Cincinnati: St. Anthony Messenger Press, 1980.

Walsh, Eugene A., S.S. *The Theology of Celebration.* Glendale, Arizona: Pastoral Arts Associates of North America, 1977.

Chapter 3

Notes

1. Robert D. Fuller, *Adventures of a Collegial Parish* (Mystic, Conn.: Twenty-Third Publications, 1981), p. 43.

2. John Maxwell, S.D.B. *Worship in Action* (Mystic, Conn.: Twenty-Third Publications, 1981), p. 26.

3. William J. Bausch, *The Christian Parish* (Mystic, Conn.: Twenty-Third Publications, 1980), p. 220

For Further Reading

Keifer, Ralph A. *To Give Praise and Thanks.* Washington, D.C.: National Association of Pastoral Musicians, 1980.

Searle, Mark, ed. *Parish: A Place for Worship.* Collegeville, Minn.: The Liturgical Press, 1980.

Chapter 4

Notes

1. "The Chicago Declaration of Christian Concern," in *Challenge to the Laity* (Huntington, Ind.: Our Sunday Visitor, 1980), p. 21.

2. Mark Gibbs, "The Development of the Laity," *Parish Ministry*, September-October 1980, p. 7.

For Further Reading

Allen, Thomas. *Liturgical Lay Ministers: A Handbook for Ministers of Bread and Cup, Music, Hospitality, Word.* Mystic, Conn.: Twenty-Third Publications, 1982.

_____. *Liturgical Lay Ministers Training Program.* 6 filmstrips, cassettes or records, study guide. Mystic, Conn.: Twenty-Third Publications, 1981.

Geaney, Dennis J., O.S.A. *Full Church, Empty Rectory.* Chicago: Fides/Claretian, 1980.

Gibbs, Mark. *Christians With Secular Power.* Philadelphia: Fortress Press, 1981.

Hovda, Robert W. *There Are Different Ministries.* Washington, D.C.: The Liturgical Conference, 1981.

Touchstones for Liturgical Ministries. Washington, D.C.: The Liturgical Conference, 1978.

Chapter 5

Notes

1. Address to Federation of Diocesan Liturgical Commissions, 1981.

2. Marty Meyer, *Goal Setting For Liturgy Teams* (Chicago: Liturgy Training Publications, 1980).

For Further Reading

Bennett, Arlene, R.S.N., ed. *Resources One: Implementation Guide for Parish Worship Committees with Strategies for Effective Liturgy Meetings.* Detroit: Dept. of Christian Worship, 1981.

Cassa, Yvonne; and Joanne Sanders. *Groundwork: Planning Liturgical Seasons.* Chicago: Liturgy Training Publications, 1982.

Huck, Gabe. *Liturgy with Style and Grace.* Chicago: Liturgy Training Publications, 1980.

Meyer, Marty. *Goal Setting for Liturgy Teams.* Chicago: Liturgy Training Publications, 1981.

Walsh, Eugene A., S.S. *The Order of the Mass: Guidelines.* Glendale, Ariz.: Pastoral Arts Associates of North America, 1979.

Chapter 6

Notes

1. Bishops' Committee on the Liturgy, *Music in Catholic Worship*

(Washington, D.C.: United States Catholic Conference, 1972), par. 23.

2. Nathan Mitchell, O.S.B., "The Changing Role of the Pastoral Musician," *Pastoral Music,* June-July 1978, p. 14.

3. *Ibid.*, p. 13.

For Further Reading

Bishops' Committee on the Liturgy. *Music in Catholic Worship.* Washington, D.C.: United States Catholic Conference, 1972.

Deiss, Lucien. *Spirit and Song of the New Liturgy.* Cincinnati: World Library Publications, 1976.

Funk, Virgil, ed. *Music in Catholic Worship: The N.P.M. Commentary.* Washington, D.C.: National Association of Pastoral Musicians, 1982.

Huck, Gabe; and Funk, Virgil, eds. *Pastoral Music in Practice.* Chicago and Washington, D.C.: Liturgy Training Publications and National Association of Pastoral Musicians, 1981.

The Ministry of Music. Washington, D.C.: The Liturgical Conference, 1979.

Pastoral Music. Washington, D.C.: National Association of Pastoral Musicians (bimonthly magazine).

Chapter 7

Notes

1. James A. Hickey, *Let Us Give Thanks to the Lord Our God* (Cleveland: Office for Pastoral Ministry, 1981), p. 14.

2. Bishops' Committee on the Liturgy, *Environment and Art in Catholic Worship* (Washington, D.C.: United States Catholic Conference, 1977), ch. 4.

3. *Constitution on the Sacred Liturgy,* par. 30., in *The Documents of Vatican II.* (New York: Guild Press/America Press, 1966) p. 148.

For Further Reading

DeSola, Carla. *Learning Through Dance.* New York: Paulist Press, 1974.

Hickey, James A. *Let Us Give Thanks to the Lord Our God.* Cleveland: Office for Pastoral Ministry, 1981.

Searle, Mark. "On Gestures." *Liturgy 80* 13 (January/February) 1982.

Chapter 8

Notes

1. John Buscemi, "Environment and Art," *Liturgy 80* 11 (November-December 1980): 2.

2. *Ibid.*, p. 5.

3. Bishops' Committee on the Liturgy, *Environment and Art in Catholic Worship* (Washington, D.C.: United States Catholic Conference, 1977), pp. 21–24.

For Further Reading

Broderick, Virginia, and Batholmew, Judi. *How to Create Banners.* Northport, N. Y.: Costello Publishing Co., 1977.

Brown, Bill, A.I.A. ed. *Building and Renovation Kit for Places of Catholic Worship.* Chicago: Liturgy Training Publications, 1982.

Buscemi, John. *Liturgical Environment, Hospitality, and the Sunday Assembly.* Barrington, Ill.: Norwest Communications, 1981 (cassette).

Wetzler, Robert, and Helen Huntington. *Seasons and Symbols.* Minneapolis: Augsburg Publishing Co., 1962.

Wolfe, Betty. *The Banner Book.* New York: Morehouse-Barlow, 1974.

Chapter 9

Note

1. Ralph E. Keifer, "Reading as Liturgical Action," *The Reader as Minister* (Washington, D.C.: The Liturgical Conference, 1980), p. 33.

For Further Reading

Practical Suggestions for Celebrating Sunday Mass. Glendale, Ariz.: Pastoral Arts Associates of North America, 1978.

Smith, Gregory F., O. Carm. *The Ministry of Ushers.* Collegeville, Minn.: The Liturgical Press, 1981.

Chapter 10

Notes

1. General Instruction to the Roman Missal (par. 5), in *The Liturgy Documents* (Chicago: Liturgy Training Publications, 1980).

2. Ralph A. Keifer, "Herald of a New Reformation," *Commonweal,* 3 July 1981, p. 401.

For Further Reading

Hovda, Robert W. *Strong, Loving, and Wise—Presiding in Liturgy.* Washington, D.C.: The Liturgical Conference, 1976.

Simons, George F. *Faces and Facts.* Chicago: ACTA, 1977.

Chapter 11

Note

1. Ralph E. Keifer, "Reading as Liturgical Action," *The Reader as Minister* (Wasington, D.C.: The Liturgical Conference, 1980), p. 28.

For Further Reading

Allen, Horace T., Jr., ed. *The Reader As Minister.* Washington, D.C.: The Liturgical Conference, 1980.

Celebrating Liturgy. Chicago: Liturgy Training Publications, 1982 (weekly notes on oral interpretation of Sunday scriptures, cycle B).

Lectionary for Mass: Introduction. Washington, D.C.: United States Catholic Conference, 1982.

Lonergan, Ray. *A Well-Trained Tongue: Workbook for Proclaimers.* Chicago: Liturgy Training Publications, 1982.

Meyer, Marty. *At Home with the Word.* Chicago: Liturgy Training Publications, 1983 (weekly questions for reflection and discussion of Sunday scriptures, cycle C).

Tate, Judith. *Manual for Lectors.* Dayton: Pflaum Press, 1975.

Chapter 12

Notes

1. Mark Searle, "Below the Pulpit," *Assembly,* November 1980, p. 10.

2. Nikos Kazantzakis, *The Saviors of God* (New York: Simon and Schuster, 1960), pp. 100, 103.

3. Searle, "Below the Pulpit," p. 105.

4. Pope Paul VI, *The Directory for Masses with Children,* par. 24.

5. James H. Provost, "Laity in the Pulpit," *America,* December 1, 1979, p. 348. Reprinted with permission of America Press, Inc., 106 West 56th St., New York, N.Y. 10019. © 1979 all rights reserved.

6. Robert McLaughlin, "Preaching," *Upturn* (Assocation of Chicago Priests), March-April 1981, p. 6.

7. Larry Ragan, "Some Ideas About Improving Communication from the Pulpit," *The Ragan Report,* August 17, 1981, p. 1.

For Further Reading

Achtemeir, Elizabeth. *Creative Preaching.* Nashville: Abingdon Press, 1980.

Babin, David. *Week In—Week Out.* New York: Seabury Press, 1977.

Burke, John, O.P. *Gospel Power.* New York: Alba House, 1977.

Chapter 13

Notes

1. Joseph M. Champlin, *An Important Office of Immense Love* (New York: Paulist Press, 1979), pp. 64–66.

2. *Immensae Caritatis* ("Facilitating Sacramental Communion in Particular Circumstances") January 1973, in Champlin, *Important Office,* p. 15.

3. Tad Guzie, *Jesus and the Eucharist* (New York: Paulist Press, 1974).

For Further Reading

Belford, William J. *Special Ministers of the Eucharist.* New York: Pueblo Publishing Co., 1979.

Champlin, Joseph M. *An Important Office of Immense Love.* New York: Paulist Press, 1979.

Kay, Melissa, ed. *It Is Your Own Mystery.* Washington, D.C.: The Liturgical Conference, 1979.

Chapter 14

Notes

1. Tissa Balasuriya, *The Eucharist and Human Liberation* (Maryknoll, N.Y.: Orbis Books, 1979), p. 2.

2. Catholic Committee on Appalachia, *This Land Is Home to Me,* Prestonsburg, Ken., 1975.

For Further Reading

Balasuriya, Tissa. *The Eucharist and Human Liberation.* Maryknoll, N.Y.: Orbis Books, 1979.

Haughton, Rosemary. *Mass—Symbol.* Barrington, Illinois: Norwest Communications, 1981. (cassette).

Hovda, Robert W. "The Mass and Its Social Consequences." *Liturgy 80* 13 (June-July 1982).